The Run of the River

THE RUN OF
THE RIVER

Mark Hume

NEW STAR BOOKS
VANCOUVER
1992

New Star Books Ltd.
2504 York Avenue
Vancouver, B.C.
V6K 1E3

Henderson Book Series No. 18
Published in association with the Canadian Parks and Wilderness Society. The Henderson Book Series honours the kind and generous support of Mrs. Arthur T. Henderson, who made the series possible.

Publication of this book is made possible by grants from the Canada Council and the Cultural Services Branch, Province of British Columbia

Maps: Gaye Hammond

Printed and bound in Canada by The Alger Press
2 3 4 5   96 95 94 93 92

Canadian Cataloguing in Publication Data
Hume, Mark, 1950-
    The run of the river

    Includes bibliographical references and index.
    ISNB 0-921586-00-0
    1. Rivers — British Columbia. 2. Water — Pollution — Environmental aspects — British Columbia.   I. Title.
TD227.B7H84 1992   363.73'94'09711   C92-091239-7

Contents

Introduction 1

THE 17 YEAR CICADA
The Columbia 3

INGENIKA DROWNING
The Peace 27

AN ACCEPTABLE LEVEL OF CERTAINTY
Taking Down the Nechako 37

MOON IN ITS HOUSE
The Thompson 61

SWIMMING AT NIGHT
The Deadman 79

EXTINCTION AND THE GENETIC CODE
The Salmon and Adams 97

THE GREAT RIVER
The Stikine 113

THE COLOUR OF COPPER
The Tatshenshini 131

VALLEY OF THE GRIZZLIES
The Khutzeymateen 153

THE RIVER GUARDIANS
The Cowichan 167

THE WAY THE WORLD WAS
The Megin 185

Selected Bibliography 206
Index 212

For Maggie, Emma, and Claire

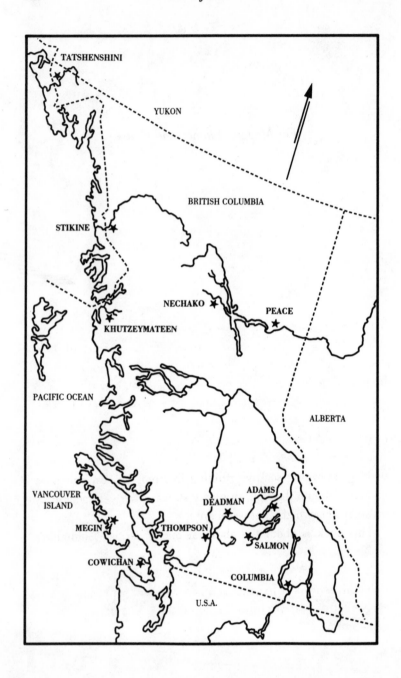

Introduction

The things I have seen in British Columbia while researching this book have been incredible: great rift valleys lying in darkness except for a single mountain wall lit by a beam of incandescent sunlight; glaciers as blue as sapphires; steelhead with such neon colours they reminded me of Amazonian parrots. I have seen rivers where the water was luminous and others so heavy with silt that you couldn't see your boots when you were standing only ankle deep. I have watched water turn red with a flood of spawning sockeye running in from the sea, and have waded for hours through an empty stream where extinction lay on every gravel bed. That was a sad day.

This book is about the abuse of one of British Columbia's most valuable resources — its rivers.

It holds lessons for all of us, for what is happening to British Columbia's rivers is happening, or has already happened, to rivers around the world, from the Rio Grande in Patagonia to the Seine in Paris.

1

Rivers tie the mountains to the sea. On Canada's western edge, they send back to the ocean, through an infinitely complex system, the rain that was drawn up from the Pacific and showered down on forested slopes and granite peaks.

Rivers spin our turbines, powering industry and lighting the cities. They carry away our industrial and residential waste. But they do not wash away our sins.

Long before the environmental stress on a river becomes obvious to most of us, it shows up in the fish. They are canaries in a mine — but canaries that cannot sing. We must pay attention to what the fish are telling us, and to the whispering voices of our rivers, for they are speaking about our future.

≅

This book would not have been possible without the support of a great many people. I would like to thank those who shared their rivers with me, those who encouraged me (particularly Terry Glavin, who insisted I write about it all) and those whose research allowed me to see things clearly. I must also thank the editors of the Vancouver *Sun*, and David Dodge, editor of *Borealis*, for supporting my interest in rivers. I am greatly indebted to Rolf Maurer and Audrey McClellan, at New Star Books, for guiding me through.

THE 17
YEAR CICADA

The Columbia

Coming down off the top of the Rossland Range to the Columbia River there is a porcupine dead on the road, all grey and black in the evening light, head turned to the side, one paw curled under its chin. I killed a porcupine like that once, as a boy, with a bow and a homemade arrow. Shot it in the head. It didn't die quickly, so I put my boot on its nose and pulled the arrow out through the toughness of the skull plate. Shot it again, because then I had to. Dark blood came out the nostrils. You know sometimes you go too far and it's terrible when you realize you can't turn back. I stood in the empty field, wind in the trembling aspens, wishing the porcupine hadn't been deserted by the safety of the trees. I felt sad about it for years.

I saw the smelter stacks first, two giant funnels jutting above the town of Trail, then the Columbia, reflecting the last light in the sky. The Cominco lead-zinc plant towers above the town and above the river; black slag covers the river bottom below the mill for miles and right there, in the middle of town, beneath the rumbling, smoking plant, discharge pipes pour untreated waste

3

into the river. The water turns black when they are dumping a slag furnace. Mercury goes into the water and collects in the fish. The walleye get the worst of it and now are among a small group of species in British Columbia listed on government health advisory warnings. If you eat more than eight ounces a week, the delicious, tender flesh of those bronze-backed fish can make you sterile. Rainbow trout in the river contain dioxins, as do white sturgeon, kokanee, burbot and whitefish. The dioxins come from a Celgar Limited pulp mill at Castlegar and although the B.C. Ministry of Health says they're safe to eat, U.S. authorities just downstream have warned anglers to consume only small fish and to skin them first.

Just a bit below the Cominco discharge pipes, Trail Creek sneaks into the river through a concrete culvert under a nine-metre wall along the Esplanade, a strip of park with a walkway from which townsfolk like to angle. Every night, when the gas stations in Trail wash out their shops, the run-off goes down storm drains into the creek and an oil slick forms along the wall. When the light is right you can see the glimmering path it makes.

Leaning against the railing, looking down on the swirling surface, Sonny, an old man who walks with a slow shuffle and who has white stubble on his round, ruddy face, watches his float bob and dip in the current. He is holding an ancient glass rod loaded with a big, open faced, spinning reel. Below the float that he's just cast, tied to a trailing yank of transparent monofilament, a trout fly, imitating a sedge, dimples the surface film. It seems an unlikely place to fish, but Sonny is serene and confident. "I got one already," he says. His friend, who is standing by with a net tied to a long stretch of yellow rope, nods in agreement, never taking his eyes off the red-and-white plastic float. It turns this way and that in the current, then hesitates. Sonny lifts the rod and the line draws tight between the top of the wall and the top of the river. "Yep, there's one," he says, breaking into a smile as

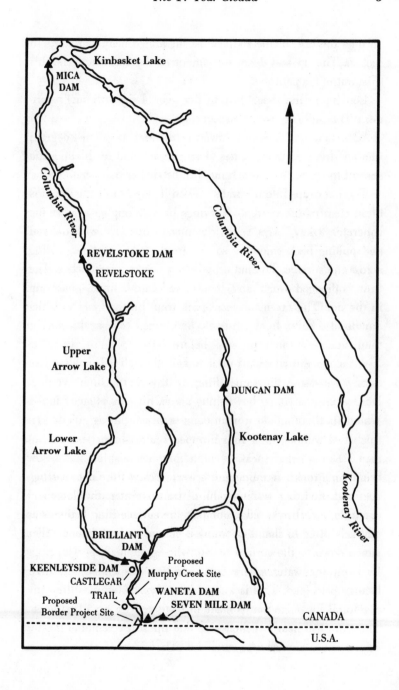

he puts the butt of the rod against his ample belly and starts to reel in. The up and down movement of the rod soon pulls his shirt out of his pants.

Looking at the sheer drop to the river, I say to Sonny's partner, "This will take some engineering."

"Oh, hell no," he says, lowering the net as a one-kilogram rainbow trout darts in flashes of silver back and forth along the base of the wall. "You watch me. It'll be slicker than snot."

The net drops into the water. When it starts to drift away, it is lifted clear of the current. It swings back, bumping against the concrete. "Okay," says Sonny, leaning to one side with the rod and pulling back smoothly so the trout starts to plane, sliding across the surface. The net drops again. Sinks a few inches. The trout is dragged over it and, hand over hand, is lifted quickly up in the net. The net man whacks the trout on the head with the handle of a knife, frees the hook, and Sonny casts again. Slicker than snot. He'll catch two more before dark.

All along the riverbanks below and above Trail, anglers like Sonny are doing the same thing on this warm June evening. Here you see a young boy fishing alone, his ears plugged into a Walkman, there an old woman dangles a line. Sitting quietly in a thicket of willows, their rods propped against branches, are two men, their silence speaking of a long friendship, and below them, on a rock outcropping, is a young couple, the man casting, the woman sitting, watching him, not the water. Swallows and common nighthawks dive along the river collecting sedge flies that are lifting in clouds on mottled brown wings. When the flies dance down to the surface to lay their eggs, small, perfect rings form on the water where trout, drifting suspended, tilt their heads up to feed. This is known as a rise. Sometimes they will rise to take a sedge that is made of feathers, tied on a tiny hook. Then you will hear a reel clicking and the soft voice of an angler calling out to anyone who can hear: "There's one."

≊

Harry Connell parks his brand new red XLT Lariat 4X4 pickup at the side of the dirt road and makes his way slowly down the river bank. He finds a perch on a bulge of black volcanic rock and works out his fly line stiffly. Almost every evening, from May to September, Harry will come down to the river that he grew up on and which, now that he's 66, has come to mean more to him than ever before. He falls into a trance when he fishes, remembering days past, when he fished here with his kids, and remembering the big fish that the river has given to him. Sometimes he carries a chain saw with him, and before fishing he knocks down a small clearing of brush and poplar on the bank. That gives him room to fly cast. He studies the water for a long time before he clears a backcast lane, so it's in just the right place. Without knowing it, fly fishermen who wander the shoreline occasionally find themselves standing just where Harry stood, attracted by the run of the river and the opening in the shoreline that allows them to cast freely. The clearings are so neatly done as to be almost invisible.

A meticulous man who spent 43 years at the Cominco mill, Harry Connell's philosophy is that big goals are best accomplished by getting right all the small steps along the way. He started as a beaker boy at the mill, washing out glass containers for the assayers, and rose to be foreman in the zinc building, a massive, modern production facility that's one of the biggest in the world. "It was designed to put out 900 tons of zinc a day," says Harry proudly as he drives past the building that engulfs an entire city block. A sign announces in flashing lights that, on this day, production hit 932 tons. "I was there for the start up," says Harry. "It was very stressful starting up a new electrolytic plant, but we did it. We did it. After we got it working like a clock I said, 'That's it. Forty-three years. I'm out.' "

He thought that when he retired he would just coast out the

rest of his life in a stress-free zone — fishing, hunting whitetails,
driving his new 4X4. Instead, he quickly found himself emerging
as a galvanizing force in a movement to save the Columbia, a
river that in B.C. is second in discharge volume only to the
Fraser and is twice the size of the mighty Peace. Just upstream
and downstream from Trail, in places where he has built foot-
paths and cleared backcast lanes, in places he has fished for 60
years, B.C. Hydro has marked off two dam sites. The provincial
hydroelectric giant wants to drown Harry's river.

Dams are old news in the Kootenays, where the Corra Linn
(1932), Brilliant (1944), Waneta (1954), Duncan (1967), Keenleyside (1969), and Seven Mile (1980) dams are as much a part of
the landscape as the rugged mountains. They stop the big rivers
from going into flood — as the Columbia did in June 1948
when it blew out the town of Vanport, Oregon, killing 41 people
— and they provide power for the industries that make the Pacific Northwest prosper. The huge Cominco smelter was built in
Trail largely because cheap hydropower was available. And not
far upstream, Celgar built a sprawling pulp mill at Castlegar for
the same reason. A lot of people, however, feel the Kootenay region has given enough to the B.C. economy, and the last
free-flowing section of the Columbia, 55 kilometres between Castlegar and Trail, should be left alone.

≈

The Columbia River rises in the Rocky Mountain Trench, a
great, flat rift valley 140 kilometres to the east of Trail. The river
runs north along a gentle gradient, sided by marshes in the rain-
shadow of the Rockies on the east bank, and fed by streams
tumbling from the Purcells to the west. It is a meandering river,
showing little sign of its dramatic potential. At Kinbasket Lake, a
dead-zone reservoir that was flooded by the Mica Dam in 1973,
inundating 28,000 hectares of unlogged forest, it hooks around
south to Revelstoke, where it hits another dam. Kinbasket stands

as a monument to industrial short-sightedness. The timber left to rot could have kept a pulp mill going for 30 years; the uncollected debris floated to the surface, making boating hazardous; the new reservoir cut off bear and ungulate migration routes, flooded 1600 hectares of wetlands and 364 hectares of meadows and, by some estimates, caused the deaths of 2000 moose and 3000 black bears. With the lake drawn down as much as 45 metres each year so power can be generated in the U.S., local residents, who have never been compensated, find themselves cut off from the water by expanding mud flats.

After the dam at Revelstoke, the Columbia pours into the Arrow Lakes, which in turn are contained by the Keenleyside Dam at Castlegar. The lakes, which stand end to end joined by a narrow neck of water, were once two of the most beautiful bodies of water in the province. They are now marred by a bathtub ring of bare rock and gravel caused by fluctuating surface levels. The Arrow Lakes also once supported large populations of huge rainbow trout, Dolly Varden and kokanee. The dams above and below the lakes destroyed the fishery. No estimates of fish losses were made at the time the dams were built, and it was learned only later that most of the trophy rainbows, fish that topped seven kilograms (15 pounds), spawned upstream of the Mica Dam, which was built without a fish ladder. Estimates have been made of fishery losses attributable to just one dam — the Revelstoke, built in 1979 — which inundated 150 kilometres of the Columbia, plus 200 kilometres of tributary streams utilized by Arrow Lakes fish. The damage: yearly losses of 4000 adult Dolly Varden, 1000 rainbow trout and 500,000 kokanee. A hatchery was built at Hill Creek, on Upper Arrow Lake, but it is unlikely it will ever restore the system to its natural abundance. According to catch statistics recorded at Olson's Marina between 1980 and 1986, not a single rainbow over 4.5 kilograms was brought in. Once they had been common. The Dolly Varden catch for the lakes stood at over 2000 in 1979, the year Revelstoke Dam was built. A graph shows a precipitous decline began in 1980, falling to almost zero by 1986. One biologist reported that Dolly Varden were no longer showing up at the base of Revelstoke Dam, where they had been netted for egg collection as they gathered in futile efforts to reach spawning grounds above. "The dam's true impact on the catchable adult population in the reservoir has now become a harsh reality," states the report. Not far to the east, at the base of the Duncan Dam, fisheries officials only learned about a run of big rainbow trout when they saw them jumping out of the plunge pool, smacking their heads against the concrete. The run soon became extinct. In an attempt to save a genetic sample of those big fish, which ran up from Kootenay Lake, some of the trout were captured so their offspring could be released in an alpine lake that was previously barren.

At the foot of the Arrow Lakes, below Keenleyside Dam, under the shadow of a dramatic rock bluff called the Lion's Head, the Columbia is reborn in the tail race in a roar of white water. From there the river runs free, becoming briefly the great river it once was, winding between dry, forested mountains, dropping through Big and Little Tin Cup Rapids, Kootenay Rapids, China Rapids, passing through Trail, and going on to the U.S. border, 55 kilometres south. Across the border the river turns through Deadman's Eddy, a place where the water slows so much that drifting bodies will drop out of the current. Soon after that the river is contained in Roosevelt Lake. After leaving Canada it runs free only once more, for 83 kilometres at Hanford Reach, where most of America's nuclear waste is stored on a riverside reservation that, in the past, has seeped into the river. Today, with the exception of the brief runs at the headwaters, Trail and Hanford, the Columbia is a series of hydro impoundments stretching its entire 2000-kilometre length.

The dams that corral the river are part of the Columbia River

Treaty, an international deal ratified after years of negotiation in the early 1960s. Under the treaty, Canada agreed to control the flow of the upper Columbia, providing massive water storage in return for a share of the extra downstream power generated. Three Canadian treaty dams, Duncan, Keenleyside and Mica, together with the Libby Dam in Montana, on the northward flowing Kootenay River, made it possible for downstream American dams to produce 2800 more megawatts of capacity. Canada initially sold the surplus power to the U.S. under a 30-year agreement, but starting in 1998 plans to reclaim it. The B.C. government, which was paid $254 million in advance, estimated in 1991 that its profit from the treaty would be $1 billion. An impressive sum — but not a complete one because the full environmental loss was never tabulated and adequate compensation funds were never paid.

By 1975 the Columbia River Power System consisted of 28 dams that produced more than 13,000 megawatts of low-cost electricity and regulated vast stretches of river to provide flood control and more efficient power generation. The dams also cut off vast amounts of spawning habitat for salmon, trout and steelhead in the river and its tributaries above Grand Coulee Dam. The Grand Coulee, in northeastern Washington, is the last dam on the mainstem before the Canadian border. It exterminated roughly half the Columbia's massive salmon runs. Before dams, about 10 million to 16 million salmon returned each year to the river. After dams, about 2 million came back annually. Over a 50-year period then, roughly 550 million salmon were eradicated from the system.

In 1940, when the Grand Coulee was nearing completion, some 400,000 adult steelhead and 360,000 summer and spring chinook ran to the reaches of the mid-Columbia. Those stocks were a small percentage of the river's overall production, but were significant because they were long-running fish. How many would have gone into Canada without Grand Coulee to block them? Nobody knows. No studies were done on the fisheries resources of the upper Columbia because Ottawa regarded the river's salmon and steelhead as fish of little interest to Canada. U.S. commercial fishermen, not Canadians, harvested them off the west coast of Washington and Oregon.

"Canadians weren't getting much benefit from those stocks at that time, although there was a native food fishery and a small sports fishery, which were overlooked," says Gordon Ennis, head of the Department of Fisheries and Oceans' eastern B.C. unit. Ennis says that in researching the Columbia's history he has been unable to locate any reports that tell him how many salmon and steelhead spawned in Canada, although he has heard stories of chinook and steelhead running into the Rocky Mountain Trench, and sockeye going up to Castlegar and turning into the Kootenay Lake system. But how many fish? And where exactly did they spawn? "I don't know," says Ennis. "I can't find anything on it at all."

Harry Connell and other oldtimers in Trail can remember how their fathers and grandfathers used to catch big chinook salmon and gun-metal-gray steelhead in the river right in town, where people today angle along the Esplanade. Those fish, of course, are gone now. One stock of summer chinook, that ran above where Grand Coulee came to block the way, averaged 13 kilograms (30 pounds); fish of 31 kilograms (70 pounds) were common. The stock is extinct. The big summer fish were eliminated along with lesser stocks because the huge dam — which is a staggering sight where it bars the river with a wall 167 metres high and 1200 metres wide — never had fish ladders. Three U.S. hatcheries built in partial compensation failed to keep the upstream races alive. Fourteen years after the Grand Coulee went in, Chief Joseph Dam was constructed 80 kilometres downriver, also without fish passage.

Canadian fisheries biologists believe that if those two dams had fish ladders, it might still be possible to return chinook, sockeye and steelhead to the upper Columbia. The journey downriver would be fraught with hazards — because of predators in the reservoirs (research behind one dam alone found squawfish ate two million young salmon and steelhead during one spring migration), turbines that chew up seven out of every ten fish sucked in, and lethal gas supersaturation in the plunge pools — but it would be feasible. So would a return trip. Fish ladders now bypass all the lower dams, deflector screens protect fry from many turbine intakes, and new cement lips have been built to disperse deadly gas. In 1991, Canada for the first time asked the U.S. to consider passing fish around Grand Coulee and Chief Joseph dams. If any steps are taken to bring chinook and steelhead back to the upper river they will have to be part of the Bonneville Power Administration's ongoing process to restore Columbia salmon runs.

Using $100 million annually in compensation funds drawn from hydropower profits, U.S. agencies since 1980 have been attempting to preserve and enhance the Columbia's salmon population. The goal is to double the Columbia's runs to 5 million salmon. One aspect of the rehabilitation has already had considerable success in increasing trout populations in Lake Roosevelt, the massive impoundment behind Grand Coulee. Rainbow trout introduced to the lake in the mid-1980s soon began running upstream, crossing the Canadian border to spawn on gravel bars in the free-flowing main river and to colonize side streams near Trail. Joining the wild stocks that were already well established, the "American trout" as locals began to call them, arrived in the spring and stayed until fall, helping to turn the Columbia near Trail into one of the most productive trout fisheries in North America.

"It was always good trout fishing here," says Harry Connell.

"But in the last several years we have been catching more, and bigger rainbows. It's nothing to catch a fish half a pound to one pound. There's lots of them. If you're fly fishing and you're good at it, you'll get trout of eight, ten, twelve pounds. There will be lots of two, three, and four pounders." Those are big fish by trout fishing standards, and when the sports anglers in Trail started to boast about trout like that, a lot of people just didn't believe them.

≅

Harry wheels his truck off Highway 22 between Trail and Castlegar, and bumps down a rough dirt road. He parks in a small clearing on the banks of Murphy Creek, just above where B.C. Hydro wants to build one of its dams. The creek charges through a rock garden, throwing spray into the trees. It is a white, tumultuous stream, and seems unpromising as a spawning tributary. "You just wait," says Harry, taking up position next to a plunge pool below a huge metal culvert that channels the stream under the highway.

He had stood there a few years earlier with Harvey Andrushak, head of the B.C. government fish culture section. After a lot of arm twisting, he'd convinced a skeptical Andrushak to come to the stream to see what locals felt was a spawning run of extraordinary fish. Andrushak, who had heard a lot of fish stories in his day, found about a dozen members of the Trail Wildlife Association waiting for him. He folded his arms and looked at the pipe and wondered if he was wasting his time. Then a big dark object came out of the white water, hit the torrent coming out of the culvert and was thrown violently back into the pool. "What was that?" asked Andrushak, blinking. "You just wait," said Harry Connell, while knowing smiles flickered on the faces of the men gathered near the pool. Soon another big fish launched itself, then another. For years the fishermen had been coming to watch this remarkable sight; now they were about to show something to one of the government's senior fisheries biologists. A cooler was pulled out of a pickup truck and there, in the ice, were some of the Columbia River's giant rainbows. Andrushak's mouth fell open. The fish were trophy size. Behind him a five-kilogram trout leaped clear of the water and disappeared up the culvert. He didn't need any more convincing, and after an electroshocking survey confirmed the obvious, he wrote a report calling the Columbia one of the most productive rivers in the province.

"The proposed Murphy Creek Dam would have a catastrophic impact on the presently productive Columbia River fishery," his report stated. "All of the current river fishery would be lost only to be replaced by a run-of-the-river reservoir similar to the Waneta, Brilliant and Revelstoke reservoirs. Such reservoirs are not capable of supporting even modest fisheries. In other words what would be lost with the Columbia River fishery would not be anywhere near replaced by the Murphy reservoir. Recent studies on a similar reservoir at Site I on the Peace River also suggest that stocking does not result in a very good fishery. Furthermore if salmon and steelhead can be routed around the Grand Coulee the river must remain undammed if there is to be any spawning habitat for these fish.

"The Columbia River from Castlegar to the border currently supports the most productive fishery for rainbow trout found in any river in B.C. There is considerable potential for increased use on the river and [it] is a logical site for increased tourism. I can envision river operated tours and guide services for rainbow trout fishing not found in many other places in B.C. If steelhead and chinook salmon were also present the economic spinoffs would be enormous. Even if a fishery for the salmon were not possible due to small numbers the tourist potential would still be significant (e.g. viewing of spawning salmon is very popular). Furthermore, if steelhead were present then the obvious step to take is to bypass the Brilliant Dam so that they could utilize the Slocan River."

When both the Canadian and provincial governments failed to act to enhance the Columbia fishery, local people took it upon themselves to do something. The Trail Wildlife Association put in hundreds of volunteer hours to make Murphy Creek more acessible to spawning trout. By moving huge boulders around, the volunteers built two pools that stepped up to the culvert, giving fish a better chance to pass the barrier. It is a small and somewhat crude attempt to help the fish. As we stood there watching the plunging white water, we could see three-kilogram trout finning in the current. At nearby Blueberry Creek, volunteers attacked a concrete tunnel passing under a railway line. They slowed down the current inside the tunnel with concrete barricades that are normally used to keep speeding cars from leaving the highway. The barricades, anchored in place, work like a series of baffles, deflecting the raging spring torrent and creating calm backwaters where trout can rest.

"Sure, it feels good to do something like this," says Harry, watching the fish in their dark spawning colours. "But it's very frustrating too. In the East Kootenays between the dams and water taxes the government gets hundreds of millions of dollars. But nothing comes back into this country for fisheries. It really gets me. We have all the ingredients. We have the fish. We have the water. We need the spawning beds. We need some money to work with. And we need to stop those dams. We'll lose the whole kit and caboodle if the dams go in."

Since retiring, Harry has been working full time to organize protests against the dams. He has been pushed on by Greg and Alphonse Mallette, two young local men who came home from university in the summer to join the fight. Greg, a graduate student at the University of Waterloo's faculty of environmental studies, did his master's thesis on the Columbia's sport fishing value, estimating it could be worth $5 million a year. Alphonse, a Ph.D. student in political science at Simon Fraser University, became a media lobbyist who would regale reporters with stories of swimming in the Columbia and feeling the pulse of the river as water was released from the dams. The vibrant young Mallette brothers seemed to be odd partners for someone as laid back as Harry, but their love of the river bridged the generation gap that lay between them.

"People say: 'Why you, Harry? Why're you getting involved? Let the younger guys do it,' because, you know, I'm 66 this month," said Harry. "Well, damn it, I've got a lot of life, a lot of memories on this river. I raised my boys here. I go along and see the places we used to go and I remember those times. And now they want to drown all that."

Harry Connell often goes fishing by himself along the Columbia. He likes to go in the evenings, when the wind drops and the sedges start to flit along the surface, bringing up the big trout. He carries a pocket full of hand-tied flies, sometimes a chain saw, and a lot of memories. When he's out there, and the thick-bodied, silver rainbows are taking his offerings, he thinks about how awful it would be if the river were turned into reservoirs between Trail and Castlegar.

"It kind of grows inside you. It's like the fish are saying: 'Harry, we're here. We need help.' So I've got to help, don't I?"

For a while we stood on the black rocks looking down at the Columbia. It was one of Harry's favourite fishing spots, and you could see why. Deer tracks marked the soft earth up the bank behind us, trees muffled the sound of the highway, and the falling line of a ridge blocked any sight of Cominco. We couldn't smell Celgar. A big eddy, moving like a revolving door in the mainstream of the current, brought fish within casting range.

"You can see them coming in with the eddy," said Harry. "You have a chance to get off two or three casts and then they drift out again." He looked upstream. "That's where they want to put the Murphy Creek Dam, right there. I can hardly believe it."

The Murphy Creek project, located about three kilometres upstream of Trail, would consist of an earth/rock dam and a
powerhouse. It would contain five generating units capable of
supplying 1625 million kilowatt-hours per year. The Border facility, to be built just above the U.S./Canada divide, would be a
twin. Between the two the entire 55-kilometre stretch of free-flowing Columbia would be impounded, the river fishery destroyed,
and access to spawning creeks like Blueberry and Murphy would
be cut off. Powerlines would run up over the big green mountainsides where whitetails live beside the river.

≅

Ralph Horney kills the 35-horsepower Evinrude outboard
and lets his 15-foot tin boat float freely with the current. Below
him the river splits violently around Big Rock, forming a standing
whirlpool to the right and pouring through a narrow, unpassable
chute on the left. Dressed in a camouflage jacket worn over a
camouflage fishing vest, he glowers at the river. "We'll be okay,"
he says after a moment, then starts to root around in a fly box.
The boat moves toward the narrow chute, then spins slowly and
begins to go upstream, drawn by an eddy. It is taking Horney, a
printer for the Trail *Times* and an expert fly tier, exactly where he
wants to go. "Fish will start rising in 30 minutes," he announces,
measuring the distance the sun has to travel to hit the tree tops.
Twenty-eight minutes later, fish begin to roll in the slick surface
windows that open briefly in the current. Sedges flutter out from
riverbank cover to tempt the trout. "There's a long apprentice-
ship fishing on this river. When I started, for about three
months I didn't fish. I just sat and watched the water. Then I began to understand what was happening. Now when I see a fish
rise, I can tell where he'll rise next. This type of fishing, the fish
doesn't have much time to look at the fly. Shape is important —
and you have to put the fly right where the fish is. There's some
coming in that eddy to your right."

Luckily the rod is loaded, with just enough line trailing on the surface to go right to a false cast. There are several loops held loose in my left hand. The rod moves through the air quickly; I see the fish, three of them, head and shoulders rising together like porpoises; throw the line. The fly settles gently. The three fish come together again; the middle one takes down the fly. I lift the rod and feel an electric connection. The line hums. The fish is powerful in the current. I turn him before he makes the chute. Wrestle him in. Slip a hand under him. Pull out the barbless hook. It's a trout, nearly two kilograms. Nothing special on the Columbia. "One night right here I had a seven-pound fish on the seat in a net. I stopped to light a cigarette, saw a rise, cast: matched pair. That's the Columbia. We can't let them build those dams. We just can't. If they build those dams they'll just create two cesspools. One for Celgar, one for Cominco. This section of the river right here will be gone forever."

Fishing on the lower river, drifting from eddy to eddy, Kerry McIntyre and Bob Mitchell are exploring every likely seam in the current. They fish in separate boats, but stay in touch with hand-held radios. When the batteries die, they just shout. McIntyre, who works producing zinc for Cominco, started fly fishing just a few years ago. He is intense, watching the water carefully and casting with pinpoint accuracy. When he sees a fish he usually takes it. Mitchell, a heavy-equipment operator, has a more laid-back style. He tells jokes ("If you fall in, don't worry. I'll know where to find you later. Deadman's Eddy"), lets his gaze wander. But when a big fish rises he becomes more predatory, leaning forward, casting with urgency. They don't kill their trout, just catch them to hold and admire, then let them go. Mitchell used to catch a lot of big walleye. He'd take them home because they were such good eating. One day he ferried some biologists up and down the river as they took fish tissue samples. "One of them told me: 'You can eat these walleyes, but do that kid of yours a favor — make sure he doesn't eat any.' Mercury can make you sterile. So's I went home; I had 20 pounds of walleye in the freezer and I threw it all in the garbage. That made me mad as hell. Nobody's got the right to pollute. And those dams? The power's going to the States. They're going to wreck our river for that?"

Just downstream from Harry Connell's fishing rock, neighbours Dale Pedersen and Jim Crispin are looking at the river, trying to imagine the changes that might take place in their own backyards. From their houses in Rivervale Junction they would be able to see the top of the Murphy Dam. On a windy day, spray from the tail race would fall on their back lawns. The two men have worked together to terrace the riverbank below their homes, and they pull their small aluminum boats up on the beach just a few yards apart. Crispin is retired, a 30-year Cominco man who worked in the zinc sulphide plant. He's been trying to think of somewhere to move but can't think of any place better than where he is now. Pedersen is a shift foreman at Cominco, running a 30-man crew. He stopped in at the plant 20 years ago when he was passing through town with his dad, and filed a job application. They asked him to start the next day. He said he was going fishing for two weeks first, then he'd start. "It's great, I love it," he says of his work. He loves the river more. If it ever came to a choice between closing the Cominco plant or losing the river, he'd vote for closing the plant. His managers think he's nuts when he says that, but they don't understand the river.

Crispin and Pedersen push off their boats and follow each other upstream, weaving through the big eddies that churn like wheels inside wheels. Crispin likes to fish Little Slough Eddy, just down and across from where he went to his high school graduation beach party in 1945. Pedersen is often in sight, upstream at Big Slough Eddy, where he saw a cougar kill a deer on the bank above him one night. Here the river is wild, the way it was from the Rockies to the Oregon coast when David Thompson explored it in 1811, meeting along the way the Lakes, Indians who marked their graves with river stones and buried their dead facing downstream, like dead salmon. Geese fly low over the water. The river and the big lakes above it are important migration staging areas for tundra swans, Canada geese, and ducks, particularly redheads. Baltimore orioles show brilliant flashes of orange as they flit through the trees. Rocky Mountain elk, caribou from the isolated Selkirk herd (the most southerly caribou population in Canada), black bears, sometimes grizzlies, mule deer and whitetails frequent the high ridges and flats above the river. The river is at the centre of the highest nesting concentration of ospreys in North America. Red-necked grebes, a species of "special concern" because conversion of wetlands has robbed it of many breeding areas, nest along the shore. As we sit in Pedersen's boat, waiting for the fish to start rising, a pair of spotted sandpipers fly past with stiff, fluttering wing beats. The birds are hunting insects among the shoreline gravel and rocks, nodding and teetering constantly, emitting a series of peet-weet notes that ring out clearly over the sound of rushing water.

"I used to bring the kids up here to see geese and sandpiper nests," says Pedersen, watching the birds. "I marked the spots with sticks so I could find them. The kids wanted to watch the babies grow up. But the dams raise the water levels overnight and flush out the nests. That's not the sort of thing you want your kids to see. I stopped bringing them to the nests after a while." Under the fluctuating water regime, the river's face changes without warning, responding to power demands. Gravel bars emerge and disappear. Birds find their dry land nests floating away; trout spawn in knee-deep water and then the redds, the gravel nests where fish eggs are laid, are dewatered, killing the eggs. Once, in a test at Priest Rapids near Hanford, U.S. authorities reduced the water so drastically that 2.6 million wild fall chinook fry died overnight. Fishermen say the changes are so sudden, so unpredictable, that you drop your anchor whenever you pull your boat ashore; sometimes the water will come up two metres while you are away for lunch, and the boat that was pulled clear of the river will be floating offshore. Whenever the water rises suddenly it means there is a surge of power generation somewhere in the system, but it also means a price is paid by the river's ecosystem — and nobody is keeping track of the cost.

Pedersen sets his boat up in Big Slough Eddy so that it drifts gently in an anti-clockwise direction, moving up along the shore before nudging towards the main current to be swept down again. With a little luck and only a few oar strokes, the boat will rotate like this in the river for hours. It is mesmerizing. As we drift we watch for trout. Sometimes they show themselves in the main current, going up as we go down. Sometimes they are behind us, going down as we go up, or in smaller eddies within the dominant eddy, spinning away in different directions. It is like fishing three rivers at once. If the fly drags, creating a wake across the surface instead of floating naturally, the fish refuse it. If a heavy leader is used, say one of over 2.7 kilograms breaking strength, the fish see it at the last moment and turn away. Big fish, fish of 4.5 kilograms or more, will often break the line, taking the fly violently. You strike, feel a surge of solid weight going against you, and then the line pops. The sudden slackness runs up your arm and into your heart.

Today there is a cool wind blowing down the river. The Rocky Mountain Trench, which extends north to the Yukon, funnels Arctic air down to southern B.C. When the cold air breaks out of the trench, it passes into the valleys of the Columbia, Elk and Kootenay rivers. In the coolness there is only a small hatch. Pedersen takes a beautiful two-kilogram rainbow. Then there is no more action. We go ashore, set the anchors up in the grass, make our way up the bank avoiding the poison ivy ("Don't piss on that; you'll be sorry," warns Crispin from experience).

Going up through the trees we listen to the vibrating buzz of cicadas. Pedersen turns back a leaf and finds one of the dark-bodied flies with transparent wings folded over its back like a tent. The insect has hatched after 17 years in the ground. It is large enough to cover my thumb from the first joint to the nail. When the cicada are falling on the water, the trout lose all caution. They rise wildly, feeding without restraint. At such times, anglers lucky enough to be on the Columbia have the best trout fishing in the world. "Sometimes you just don't know where to cast," says Pedersen. "The eddy will be full of fish, moving all around you. It's enough to give you a heart attack."

A long way up through the trees we come to a small cabin, 10 feet by 12, made of dark, squared-off tamarack 17 inches through at the butt end. Crispin remembers the cabin from when he was a boy; it was old and abandoned then and nobody knows the story of how it came to be here. When Pedersen stumbled on it, the roof was caved in and the inside was gutted. He fixed it up so his son could go there with his BB-gun and his dog. Put in some bunks and a stove. Swept the floor. One day, when Pedersen was there alone, the owner came home — a big black bear with scars on his cheek and chest, one of his eyes milky with blindness. The bear ripped at the walls until it tore a hole near the stove pipe. Pedersen was inside with an ax, shouting at the bear to go away. It was dark in the cabin, which was built without windows. A big black foreleg came through the hole, searching for him, the claws out, the rough skin on the foot pad feeling about in the air. He hit the bear and it went away. But it came back later, after Pedersen had gone, climbed onto the roof, ripped it up, went inside and destroyed all the work that had been done; smashed down the door on its way out. Next time the bear came back, Pedersen was waiting on the ridge. He killed it with one shot and has felt bad about it ever since. "I didn't want him around with my son out here," he said. "You come up in his back yard and then kill him because you want to be here. Of course you feel terrible about it." He never told his son. The cabin has been repaired. The tamarack still shows the deep scars left by the bear's claws.

The river jars things loose. Pedersen starts talking about a grizzly he killed once, up on the Arrow Lakes. It's a story he's held inside for a long time. He was bow hunting for deer when he saw the bear nine metres away, its small eyes locked on him, the silver-tipped hair on its shoulders bristling as if electricity was arcing through it. Pedersen drew his bow and hoped the bear would go away. But you can only hold a bow at full draw for so long. It's like trying to hold your breath. After a minute the pain builds up inside, spreads everywhere. If you hold it too long you start to shake, then the muscle spasms hit. Pedersen waited and thought about his life and his family. He was cold with fear. He wanted to run, but knew he couldn't. The bear would be on his back in a second. He felt his arms starting to tremble from holding the draw for so long. The bear popped its jaws at him. He let the arrow go and watched it cross the space between them. It went into the bear up to the feathers. Then the grizzly charged. At three feet it passed his left side and kept running. Why didn't it kill him? Run him down and maul him? Enraged grizzlies are supposed to do that. This one ran into the forest, leaving a trail of dark blood. Pedersen stood there shaking, feeling sick. He realized that at some point he'd pulled his sheath knife and held it in front of him towards the bear. Later he found part of the arrow, bitten off, covered with blood. There was a place where the bear had stopped, blood everywhere. That was all. It breaks his heart to think about that bear. He didn't want to kill it. Didn't want it to go off into the woods alone with the shaft of a broken arrow and razor-edged hunting head moving about deep inside it. Sometimes you go too far and can't turn back.

It's like all these dams on the Columbia. Nobody wanted to kill all those fish, to eradicate millions of salmon, to cut off the big Arrow Lake rainbows from their spawning grounds. People just wanted cheap hydropower and weren't thinking very far ahead. Now you've got to ask yourself, do we want to stop before the last of the Columbia is drowned? Have we learned anything yet?

Going back to the river, someone plucks a sleeping cicada from a leaf, puts it on a hook and casts it on the water. There is a huge swirl and the cicada is gone. We float back down the river in early darkness, pull the boats up on the glacial sand below Pedersen's house. He looks at the water sadly and says, "Sure is going to be a shame when they dam this bastard. That's all a guy can think about."

≈

If dams must be built to provide power for British Columbia's growing needs, then it makes environmental sense to build them on rivers that have already been impounded, instead of destroying pristine watersheds. But that argument does not hold true for the Columbia River near Trail.

Although the Columbia has probably been dammed more than any other river in North America, perhaps in the world, the last free-flowing section in Canada is still a remarkable stretch of water. It deserves protection.

The environmental and social costs of the Murphy Creek and Border dams would be too high. The river supports what is B.C.'s most productive rainbow trout fishery and is the cornerstone of a local angling culture that has a long history. Nobody has the right to take that away from the people of the Kootenays, who have lost so much of their natural heritage already, providing cheap power to the rest of the province.

With spawning habitat enhanced in tributary streams between

Trail and Castlegar, with more environmentally sensitive operation of the Keenleyside Dam and the possible addition of fish
ladders, the Columbia River in southern B.C. could become the
greatest trout stream on the continent. Furthermore, if Ottawa
presses U.S. authorities to build fish ladders on the Grand Coulee and Chief Joseph dams, then salmon and steelhead will one
day return to spawn in the Columbia near Trail.

The Bonneville Power Administration is spending $100 mil-
lion a year in an attempt to restore the Columbia's once-great
salmon runs south of the border. That is a figure worth pondering while we consider how much the river is worth to Canada.

B.C. Hydro has been trying to compensate the Arrow Lakes
through a small hatchery and, in 1991, joined with the provincial Ministry of the Environment in announcing a $1 million
program aimed at "reestablishing fish and wildlife" in the Columbia River Basin, with Kinbasket Reservoir as a starting point.
B.C. Hydro has adopted a new environmental ethic for the
1990s which suggests it wants to take responsibility for the damage its dams have caused. But it has a long way to go. The power
corporation should follow the example set by the Bonneville
Power Administration and establish a permanent environmental
contingency fund that is supported by a percentage of annual
profits. The environmental problems created by hydropower generation in this province will not be fixed by a million dollars here
or there. It will take a long-term commitment of hundreds of millions of dollars.

It's time B.C. Hydro — and the people of the province — began to make a serious effort to repair the environmental damage
done by its dams, not just in the Kootenays, but throughout British Columbia. Power has a price — and unless the full
environmental costs are factored in, we are just cheating ourselves and robbing future generations.

INGENIKA
DROWNING

The Peace

Behind the dam the river backed up into the lake and the lake backed up onto the land until it covered the beaches and covered the trees above the shore. It drowned the drumbeat of grouse, lapped up deer shadows and took to itself traplines and the teeth of pine marten. The ancestral graveyard below Ingenika village turned to mud and slid beneath the spreading surface of Williston Lake. The pine forest turned gray with death and all that was not rooted rose to the surface, including coffins from the burial ground. Along the shoreline, after the water had stopped rising, the Ingenika built a long row of campfires and wept in the darkness, for they could hear their spirits drowning.

"When we used to go along the river it was so beautiful. Come around the bend — a big moose standing. After the flood, nothing but dying animals, water and debris," said Jean Isaac, recalling the drowning of Ingenika.

The 200-member Ingenika band in northern British Columbia settled in the Finlay Trench region at least seven thousand years ago. They occupied the whole trench, nomadically drifting

from place to place for hunting, berry picking and fishing. ("Ingenika" is a Sekani word for bearberry.) They used the Finlay
River, which pours down out of the north, as a corridor to move
through the rugged country, extending their range more than
100 kilometres upstream. They travelled on the Parsnip, which
runs from the south to join the Finlay, and on the Peace, which
takes the flow of the Finlay and Parsnip east through the Rocky
Mountains. They settled down the Peace River as far as Hud-
son's Hope and used to follow the big river through the Rockies
to hunt and trade with the Cree in what is now northern Alberta.
The many bands that occupied the region were known as the
Sekani; to the south were the Carrier, who traded the Sekanis'
goods out to the coast and brought them iron from the Gitksan.
The Rocky Mountain Trench and the Finlay Trench were such remote, rugged areas that the Sekani were among the last of the
aboriginal nations to be found by European explorers in the late
1700s. For centuries after white contact, the Sekanis prided
themselves on being independent and self supporting.

In the late 1960s, as part of a huge hydroelectric project on
the Peace River, the W.A.C. Bennett Dam was built, creating
Williston Lake, the biggest reservoir in the province. It flooded
the Finlay Trench. Downstream, where the Peace flows across a
region of vast boreal forest to join the Slave, then turns north to
feed the Mackenzie, the dam has affected water levels as far
away as the Arctic Coast. By dramatically reducing spring flooding on downstream deltas, the dam changed the makeup of plant
communities. Horsetails, the mainstay of muskrat diets, began to
vanish while less productive terrestrial ecosystems rapidly advanced, unchecked by flood waters. Nobody predicted when the
dam went in that reed beds 1100 kilometres downstream would
die off, but that's what happened, and the muskrat population
soon crashed. The dam also caused water levels to increase during the winter, and again the muskrats suffered. Usually water

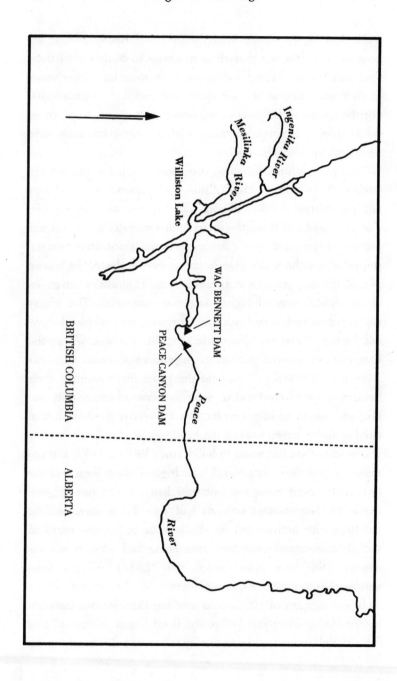

levels drop in the winter after the ice has formed, creating air pockets under the ice that allow muskrats to come out of their dens and forage. After the Bennett Dam went in, winter water levels rose, filling in the air space and trapping the muskrats. For the Cree and Chipewyan trappers on Athabasca Lake, those subtle changes meant economic hardship because muskrats were what kept their traplines going.

This was nothing, however, compared to what happened upstream of the dam, where Williston Lake spread out to devour 362 kilometres of valley bottom. For the Sekani, who in 1870 and 1890 had withstood the social impact of two significant gold rushes, the invasion of the flood waters was devastating and unstoppable. As the water rose in the reservoir, destroying native homes, hunting grounds and traplines, the Ingenika, a sub-group of the Sekani, moved higher into the mountains. The Finlay River, which had once been their pathway, became too dangerous for small boat travel because of drifting debris. Where the Cree had lost muskrat habitat, the Ingenika saw moose meadows destroyed. The valleys that held the game that sustained their hunting culture were flooded. Soon the sense of community was lost and social problems — increased poverty, alcoholism and child abuse — began to stalk the band.

The dam took five years to build, from 1962 to 1967, and the reservoir took five years to fill. The Ingenika had been told the lake level would come up, but they had no idea how high it would go. Government officials had visited the area, holding meetings with natives, but few Indians spoke English well and nobody understood what they were being told when it was announced the lake would reach the "250 level" — a term meaningless to everyone but engineers.

In the summer of 1967, band member Francis Isaac travelled up the Finlay River just before the flood began. He found that B.C. Hydro crews had been through, burning down all the Indian cabins they could find. When Isaac went back to where his people were camped at the confluence of the Finlay, Peace and Parsnip rivers, he told them what he had seen. For the first time, they became really afraid.

All that summer the water rose. The people were horrified when it reached into the forest and began swallowing the trees. They built campfires along the shore and watched what was happening.

≅

Bill Bloor, who used to run a store at Finlay Forks, went over one night to the campfires and found all the people sitting there as if at a funeral. "The older people were weeping. They were saying, 'No more good land' . . . It was a very, very sorrowful sight."

During daylight the Indian people would go out in their boats and try to rescue drowning animals. They brought in squirrels and moose calves. The big moose were too dangerous, thrashing about in panic, trying desperately to swim through the drifts of debris. They could sink a boat when they were like that.

"One time we were coming up Five Mile [creek], we heard a moose calling. Here a bull moose was caught under a tree. We chopped at it, but by the time we got it loose he had already drowned," recalled Francis Isaac.

The Ingenika saw many moose drown and heard their death calls at night. After that, for a long time, many of the hunters couldn't bring themselves to shoot moose anymore. It didn't seem right.

In 1968 the federal government established two small reserves, Tutu and Parsnip, near the new resource town of Mackenzie. There was no work there, no place to trap. But the government assumed the Ingenika people could simply walk away from the traditional economy that had sustained them for thousands of years, and somehow, overnight, adapt to a brave new world.

Some made the move to the reserves, but others dispersed, looking for new homes in the unflooded portions of the Trench. Displaced from their land and traditional way of life, the people fell into despair. For the first time, alcohol became a serious problem in the community. With alcohol abuse came all the traditional evils: sexual abuse, violence, fetal alcohol syndrome. A history prepared by the bands describes this period as "among the darkest ever experienced by the Ingenika and Mesilinka people."

Gradually, however, they began to regroup. In 1970 the Ingenika band was formally established, thus gaining a separate identity from the Finlay River band, with whom the government had lumped them. The next year, between 50 and 60 members moved to Ingenika Point, which was in an unflooded portion of their ancestral territory and was an old hunting area. Some settled in nearby Mesilinka Valley and became the Mesilinka band. The Tutu and Parsnip reserves were soon empty — and they have remained that way to this day. In 1989 the two bands began seeking reserve status for the land they had reoccupied and they produced a paper setting out their economic and social objectives, which included community-based logging shows. They also joined with the Carrier-Sekani Tribal Council (which represents bands of both the Carrier and Sekani Nations in north-central British Columbia) in launching a comprehensive land claim to their ancestral lands, including the Rocky Mountain Trench which holds the Finlay, Mesilinka and Ingenika rivers and Williston Lake.

The issue of the land claim is one thing, but quite another is the simple question of compensation for the people who were displaced by the hydro project, losing their homes, their traplines — and in some cases their families. Such a tragedy would not be tolerated today by native organizations like the now-powerful Carrier-Sekani Tribal Council. But in those days, resource developers like B.C. Hydro, and Alcan farther to the south, had little opposition.

Prior to the flood, the Department of Indian Affairs promised to compensate band members for trapline losses. Some were told they would get $1000 to $2500. A grand total of $30,000 was to be paid out and the band was told there would be further discussion once the reservoir had reached full height. The government never came back for those discussions and many band members say they never saw the initial payments that were promised. It wasn't until 1989 that the provincial government took some steps towards compensation, offering the band $1.5 million to establish a reserve at Ingenika and develop some long-term economic plans.

"We are happy to see them putting things forward in negotiations but we will say in no uncertain terms this falls far short of what an adequate settlement for reserve compensation should be," said Waldemar Braul, legal counsel for the band.

During the third annual Electrical Energy Forum held by B.C. Hydro in 1990, Ed John, hereditary chief of the Lasilyu Clan of the Tl'azt'en tribe of the Carrier Nation and former chief of the Carrier-Sekani Tribal Council, was asked what type and amount of compensation would be acceptable. He replied that, although financial settlement would help, it was not simply a question of money.

John said the Ingenika, and the Cheslatta people who were flooded out of their homes by Alcan's Nechako power project, want their sense of identity back. The floods washed away not just land and wildlife, but complete cultures, bringing an end to what the elders called "the singing days." That is what they want returned — a reason to sing again.

"They were affected very deeply by their removal from their tribal territory ... It's affected their community psyche, their community spirit in such a way that they refer to their days as preflooding days and postflooding days. Everything is measured by those concepts, and they look at where they are now and what they would like to do. When you are looking at these kinds of issues . . . it's not really just a question of financial compensation. It's far deeper than that. It's far more serious than just paying somebody off, and then saying that we've paid them off, and that's good enough."

The Indians who were flooded out to provide profit for industry and power for the province of British Columbia, may one day be healed, if society cares enough to help them. But the Ingenika, who live in a village that has no electricity, will never get back the land under the reservoir. The rich bottom land that sustained them for seven thousand years is buried forever, haunted by the ghosts of ancestors spilled from their coffins. At night, if you listen to the waves that wash ashore on Williston Lake, sometimes you can hear the unearthly calls of drowned moose.

It is stupefying that any government, even the rapacious regime of premier W.A.C. Bennett and his resources minister, Ray Williston, could lay waste the land and mistreat its people with such callous disregard. But it happened. And it appears it could happen again, for there is no widespread sense of shame in society over the drowning of Ingenika or the damming of the Nechako River or the destruction of the Arrow Lakes and the Columbia River by B.C. Hydro.

Compensation? Certainly it should be pursued, with a percentage of energy profits returned to the people who paid the price for the generation of that power. But more important than that is the establishment of a system that accepts the inherent rights of native people to self-determination. Native people must have the political power to protect themselves, and to protect the natural resources upon which their cultures are based.

In 1989 Chiefs Gordon Pierre and Ray Izony of the Ingenika and Mesilinka bands issued a statement in support of Amazon Indians fighting against the Kararo Dam on the Xingu River.

"We know what the Amazon Indians are facing and we do not wish to see them suffer the hardships we have faced for the last 20 years," they said.

"To avoid these types of hardships on indigenous peoples like us, the governments should adopt the significant recommendations of the Brundtland Commission report on the Environment and Economy. We think our own governments should strongly consider adopting the United Nations Commission recommendations that indigenous people should have a decisive say in industrial development which will affect their tribal homelands and ways of life."

How could anyone argue with that?

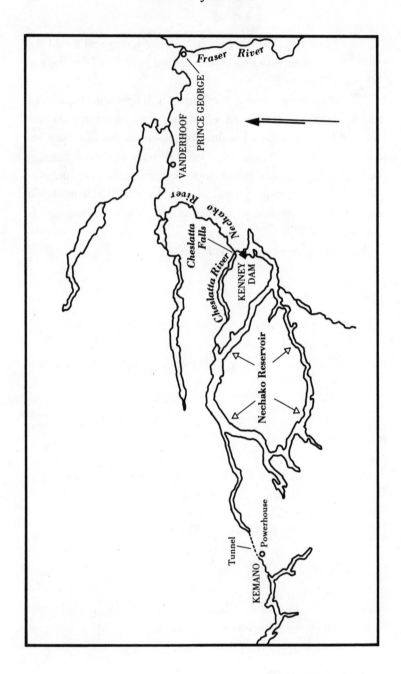

AN ACCEPTABLE
LEVEL OF
CERTAINTY

Taking Down the Nechako

"This project contains elements which make it of more vital concern to salmon than any other fish habitat question we are likely to encounter in the rest of this century."
  WAYNE SHINNERS, director of the Department of Fisheries, commenting on Alcan's proposed hydro development on the Nechako River, 1984

"I believe sincerely that we can find a way for fish and hydro-electric power to co-exist. The issue is not fish versus power. I believe we can have both."
  TOM SIDDON, Minister of Fisheries, 1987

A few days after Siddon expressed the dream of a perfect world, University of British Columbia president David Strangway chaired a closed-door meeting in which a small group of officials reached an extraordinary agreement on Alcan's Kemano Completion Project. It was decided that Alcan, which had been drawing

37

off 30 percent of the Nechako's flow to power its Kemano I
Dam, could expand the facility and drain 83 percent of the water
out of the river. The expansion would allow Alcan to add to its
Kitimat smelting plant when market conditions became favour-
able. In the meantime it could sell its surplus power to B.C.
Hydro, continuing a profitable arrangement that began in 1978.
In compensation for environmental damage, Alcan would pay for
a massive, and experimental, technological fix of the Nechako,
one of the most important salmon-producing tributaries of the
Fraser River. The plan, on a scale never before attempted in
Canada, was described as "failsafe" because if stream reengineer-
ing didn't work, Alcan would build a fish hatchery as a last line
of defence.

Siddon said the deal provided "an acceptable level of certainty" that salmon would be protected.

Despite the minister's faith, there were troubling voices of dis-
sent, raised not just by environmentalists but also by scientists
who had spent their entire professional lives studying salmon.
Among them was Dr. Don Alderdice, a retired salmon physiolo-
gist who worked for the Department of Fisheries and Oceans
(DFO) for 49 years and who contributed to a federal Nechako
Task Force report on the project. His assessment: "The Kemano
Completion flows are going to be disastrous, absolutely catastrophic."

He was publicly supported by Dr. Gordon Hartman, a retired
DFO salmon ecologist who also had worked on Kemano studies.

"If politicians said 'we have decided to write off the Nechako
in return for hydropower' I would have no problem with that,"
said Hartman. "But the government has portrayed this as a project that does not harm the Nechako salmon resources, and that
is false."

Imagine how wonderful it would be if technology could save
us, if rivers could be harnessed to generate hydropower without

trading off natural resources. The government has promised that is what will happen on the Nechako — a river that's vital to 20 percent of the salmon in the Fraser River.

≋

Every fall I make a pilgrimage to the mountain slopes above West Vancouver to watch the salmon running through the canyons into the Capilano fish hatchery. Crossing the beautiful arc of the Lions Gate Bridge, I'm reminded of how, in the 1950s, steelhead anglers fought against the Capilano's Cleveland Dam because they knew it would destroy the river. The Capilano, which had runs of wild coho, chinook and steelhead, was hard to reach in those days and although it had been dammed earlier — in 1887 when Vancouver first developed it as a water supply — key spawning beds were not ruined. The Cleveland, however, was placed just downstream of the main spawning grounds, burying the gravel under 91 metres of reservoir water. Among those who joined sports anglers in opposing the dam was the author and naturalist Roderick Haig-Brown, who said it would be worth a million dollars to preserve the Capilano salmon runs "and to perpetuate sport fishing in a stream which is so close to a giant city."

Sports anglers estimated the Capilano's pre-dam runs at 30,000 coho and 3000 steelhead, but the dam soon changed all that. The reservoir slowed downstream smolt migration, turning a two-day drift into a 23-day odyssey, and exposing the fish to increased predation. Leaving the reservoir, 57 percent of coho and 69 percent of steelhead were battered to death going down the dam's spillway. The year after construction was finished only 5000 coho and 119 steelhead came back to the base of the Cleveland, where they were caught in traps. By 1965, despite the release of artificially reared fish (which started in 1957), only 612 coho and 49 steelhead returned. There is a remnant population of steelhead in the Capilano still, 20 to 100 fish, some of which spawn naturally in the river below the hatchery. They are not the huge wild stock that once drew anglers to the canyon pools. Spring salmon are virtually extinct in spite of the hatchery's best efforts. Only 563 returned in 1991. Hatchery coho — small, genetically inferior fish that seem to have come out of a mold — do return in large numbers (37,921 in 1991), and in the fall you can look down from Lions Gate and see fishermen gathered at the mouth of the Capilano in a swarm. Just up from the estuary, members of the Capilano Indian band continue something of a traditional harvest, gaffing salmon as they run through the shallows. The women sit in cars, smoking and listening to the radio, watching the men at work.

Upstream, standing in the hatchery parking lot, you see a ribbon of coho edging through fast water below a holding pool where salmon school before taking a narrow gate that leads them into the plant. Inside the hatchery there are viewing windows. Behind the thick plates of glass the fish stack up like cord wood. Some of them have blunted noses from banging against the glass and cement. Their eyes are blank. They wait there calmly, as if they were drugged, until they are netted out by hatchery workers. Eggs and milt are squeezed from about 3000 fish, and their darkening bodies are thrown with the rest into dead fish bins. That's it. Life's over.

I'm not sure why I go to the hatchery every year, because the whole scene fills me with sadness and despair. Perhaps it is just to reaffirm what I already know: that while engineers can reproduce fish, they cannot replace nature. Hatcheries are technological marvels and they may be a necessity in the modern world, but they are not signs of progress; they are monuments to our failure to protect rivers.

In his book *Capilano — The Story Of A River*, James Morton writes that the Cleveland Dam could easily have been built farther upstream, leaving the spawning beds open to wild runs of salmon. It would have cost the City of Vancouver a few thousand dollars more in engineering costs — but officials didn't think it was worth it at the time. After all, there were a lot of wild salmon in those days. And they knew they could always build a hatchery if all else failed.

≈

To find the Nechako River you turn onto Nechako Avenue in the small central British Columbia town of Vanderhoof, and head out through the dry ranch country that spreads to the south. You can do 80 kilometres an hour on the smooth gravel road that cuts straight across the landscape. It's April, and the first geese of spring are dropping down into narrow bands of water that have opened along the lake margins. Beef cattle, stupid and ponderous, stand by the fence rows. There is bush and muskeg interspersed with hay fields and forested hills along the 60-kilometre road, which was built by Alcan in 1950 to provide access to the site of what, at the time, was the largest sloping, rock-filled, clay-core dam in the world. More than 15 million litres of gas were used in constructing the road and Kenney Dam. One proud engineer calculated that enough material was moved that if it had all been loaded in dump trucks, they could have lined up, bumper to bumper, from Vancouver to Halifax.

Those were boom days. World War II was just over and the project was tackled with a gung-ho attitude and total disregard for the environment. Harry Jonini, resident engineer for Alcan, described in a 1954 article how the dam had been built with aggressive enthusiasm. "And, finally," he concluded, "with the rising reservoir, there has been harvested an amount of water equivalent to no less than 359,000,000,000 8-ounce beer glasses! This formerly wasted water is now, thanks to the Kenney dam, available for useful services."

A similar article, compiled by Alcan's general engineering department, detailed construction of the aluminum smelter, pow-

ered by the electricity from the dam. The report described the
country as uninhabited "except for a few scattered Indian settlements," and went on to say: "the original establishment of a
beachhead from which to carry out operations was in many ways
parallel to a military landing operation." Indeed.

An ad in the *Engineering Journal* showed a huge hand reaching down out of the heavens, like the hand of God, to place a
power plant at the head of the reservoir. "They've put a heart
into a mountain," said the ad, in which the Bank of Montreal
congratulated Alcan on completing the job. "Yes, this is among
the very greatest things to happen to the West since the trans-
continental railroads were built — one of the biggest strides yet
in Canada's march to greatness."

≈

Kenney Dam is a wall of dirt and rock across a narrow gap
at the head of the Nechako Canyon. A sprawling lake system lies
on one side and what's left of the river is on the other. The dam
is terraced, like a huge Inca temple, and standing on it, straining
to hear a trickle of water in the riverbed below, you have to wonder what God you should worship here. It is silent down in the
canyon, where the river once rushed to life, spilling from a chain
of deep, glaciated lakes that stretch off west in a rough 'Y'
through the rugged Coast Range. After the dam was finished, in
1954, Ootsa, Tahtsa, Whitesail, Eutsuk, Tetachuck, Natalkuz and
Knewstubb lakes rose and merged until they basically became
one giant, sprawling reservoir, two arms of which cut through
Tweedsmuir Park. A tunnel through the mountains spilled water
into Alcan's turbines, the "heart in the mountains" which produced electricity to be used in the aluminum smelter built on
the Pacific Coast at Kitimat. Surplus power, of which there was a
lot, was later sold to B.C. Hydro. Alcan did not log the lake valleys before it started flooding, drowning a forest in the process.
Rotting vegetation made the water undrinkable.

In the 1950s the region was extremely remote, and relatively few people were witness to what was lost. Joseph Junell, a Washington resident who owns 80 acres near Ootsa, wrote a letter to DFO and Alcan, stating his dismay over what had happened to the watershed and the prospect that the level of Ootsa Lake would be raised again under Kemano Completion.

"The violence which Alcan Aluminum Limited (with full blessings of the B.C. government) wreaked upon Ootsa Lake is beyond belief. Indeed, as one looks down at the Alcan jungle, lying just beneath the water's surface, it is difficult to believe that this was once a chain of gleaming pristine lakes, bordered by beautiful stands of aspen, spruce, and pine. Staring up at you now are its remains, a mangled forest of grotesquely twisted tree trunks and limbs. Dead trees, standing like skeletons, still border the lake's edge, while on the shore line are the bleached white bones of trees that were the first to succumb to the flooding. This ugly defacement which man wrought in a short span of six or seven years will likely take nature several hundred to completely heal."

There were scars to the land — and scars to the people that lived there. When the Carrier-Sekani Tribal Council told DFO what it thought of Kemano Completion, Chief Marvin Charlie of the Cheslatta band recalled what had happened during phase one of Kemano, when the reservoir was filled. Journalist Pat Turkii recorded his story:

" 'In the 1950s my people were called to a meeting on the Cheslatta Reserve on very short notice. Some of our people were trapping and did not make it to the meeting. Those that were able to attend did not know what it was about. However, they went anyway, just to find out that they had to move from their homes immediately. Not next week, next month, or next year, but they had to move out now. Some of the elders refused to move for the love of their land. They were told that if they didn't move the law would move them. Seeing that they had no choice but to move, they did.'

"Charlie says his people were uprooted, forced out of their homes and land in April when the weather was poor. Travelling on the ice was out of the question so they were faced with a tough journey of 40 to 50 miles out to Grassy Plains on a summer trail from Cheslatta Lake. There, they camped out in tents through spring and summer.

"As a result of having to camp out in the wet weather, he said, many contracted tuberculosis. Some were lucky enough to find an empty cabin to live in until they could get farms. Some camped out as late as November before they could get land.

"In June, some of them went back to Cheslatta for furniture and other belongings, but as a result of the flooding they couldn't get to their homes.

"Two graveyards were flooded. One washed down the river. The people walked the banks in hopes of finding the bodies of their loved ones . . . only to find empty coffins floating around in the river.

" 'My people lost everything. They lost their homes, land, traplines, and most of all, their traditional territories.' "

Since 1954, the Carrier-Sekani people have suffered the continued impact of Kemano. The Cheslatta, Stoney Creek, Fort George, Broman Lake, Fraser Lake, Stellaquo, Necoslie, Tl'azt'en Nation and Takla Lake bands have faced reductions in salmon stocks caused by lower water levels and the destruction of salmon habitat in the Nechako system. The Cheslatta were forced to relocate to new reserves. Beaver and muskrat habitat dried up along the Nechako, reducing the fur harvests of the Cheslatta, Stoney Creek and Fort George bands. The Fraser Lake band faced erosion problems because of the way the Nautley River speeded up and began devouring its own bed when the Nechako dropped. The Indian people who lived in "a few scattered settlements" have not been compensated since Alcan subdued the wilderness with militaristic precision.

≅

The history of Kemano is a long and complicated one (it has been set out in substantial papers by Will Koop of the Rivers Defence Coalition and by DFO experts), but the shorthand version is simple enough. In 1947 the B.C. government, salivating at the prospect of industrial development, approached Alcan with promises of cheap hydropower. It takes huge amounts of electricity to produce aluminum, 20,000 kilowatt hours per ton, and any company with a cheap power source is ahead of the competition. One analyst has said Alcan pays 3 cents for the electricity needed to produce one pound of aluminum, while U.S. producers pay 18 cents and those in Japan pay 35 cents. Following World War II the aluminum market was booming and Alcan was looking for major expansion. B.C. offered the combined prospect of massive water diversion for power generation, and deep ocean access for bauxite shipment. And Alcan liked the political attitude in B.C. In 1949 the government brought in the Industrial Development Act, specifically to facilitate the deal. It gave Alcan incredible powers. In 1950, using the bill, Victoria granted Alcan a water license, signing over to the company the rights to completely divert the Nanika and Nechako rivers. Years later B.C.'s comptroller of water rights, Howard DeBeck, would describe the rights given Alcan as "an aberration on our books, more wide ranging than anything we've ever issued. Back in the postwar years . . . the government thought it had to hand over sweeping powers as the price it had to pay for development."

A year later, construction started on the Kenney Dam and on the smelter and townsite at Kitimat.

In addition to getting virtual ownership of the Nechako and Nanika rivers, Alcan also got mineral rights on all crown land prior to flood; timber rights on all flooded crown land, with no

stumpage charges; 14,000 acres at $1.60 an acre for industrial
and residential development at Kitimat; and unique municipal
status for all dams and facilities, effectively granting taxes to the
company. Nowhere in the deal was there any requirement for Alcan to provide enough water for the survival of fish in the rivers.
DFO officials protested weakly, but were simply ignored and so
let the matter drop — effectively abandoning Ottawa's mandate
to protect the fisheries resource.

From 1952 to 1956, Alcan turned off the Nechako, diverting
all water into the reservoir system. When the water dropped,
fisheries officers were able to walk the upper Nechako and for
the first time get a firm assessment of the river's fisheries value.
They found 4000 chinook spawning redds. The river was dry, except for downstream tributary feeds, until Alcan began spilling
excess reservoir water through Skins Lake and Cheslatta Falls,
eventually returning the river to about 70 percent of its natural
volume. This was the first phase of the Kemano hydroelectric development, and the environmental damage it caused was incalculable.

In 1979, Alcan announced it would proceed with the second
phase, Kemano Completion, which would increase diversion of
the Nechako and dam the Nanika, in order to double generating
capacity of the Kemano power plant. At the time, Alcan was already producing power surplus to its aluminum smelting needs
and was making about $1 million a month in sales to B.C. Hy-
dro, which in turn was selling the power to the U.S.

From the start Alcan said phase two was needed to facilitate a
second smelter at Kitimat, but no firm plans to expand were ever
produced. Even the aluminum workers didn't believe Alcan was
interested in doing anything more than cashing in on power
sales. Jim Nyland, a spokesman for the Smelter Union in Kitimat, said aluminum workers opposed Kemano Completion
because they believed Alcan was expanding power capacity without any intention of increasing aluminum production. "You

don't bite the hand that feeds you," Nyland said, "[but] we are skeptical. If they want us on board . . . they have to give us some concrete deadlines on when there will be a second smelter." Those deadlines never materialized — and neither will the second smelter.

Salmon runs in the Nechako were badly hurt in the 1950s during and following construction of Alcan's facilities. Throughout the 1960s and 1970s relatively high volumes of water were allowed to flow into the river because Alcan couldn't use all the available water. Salmon numbers began to improve. Then, in 1978, conditions changed markedly when Alcan saw an opportunity to start selling surplus power to B.C. Hydro. In generating that extra power, Alcan increased the diversion of Nechako water from 30 percent to 70 percent of the river's flow. Coincidentally, a series of dry weather years had begun and fisheries biologists were soon aware of a crisis on the river.

In 1980 DFO ordered Alcan to increase the flows in the Nechako. When Alcan refused, DFO got a Supreme Court injunction, setting a base flow rate sufficient for chinook salmon to spawn. The injunction was renewed yearly until 1985 while the company, DFO, and provincial officials haggled over what the flow rate should be. Failing to reach agreement, Alcan asked for a 1987 trial to determine who really had ultimate authority over the Nechako — the company or DFO. On its side, Alcan had the "full speed ahead and dam(n) the environment" water licence it signed with B.C. in 1950. On the other side, DFO had the Fisheries Act, section 20.10 of which states: "The owner or occupier of any slide, dam or other obstruction shall permit to escape into the riverbed below the said slide, dam or other obstruction, such quantity of water, at all times, as will, in the opinion of the Minister, be sufficient for the safety of fish and for the flooding of the spawning grounds to such depth as will . . . be necessary for the safety of the ova deposited thereon." Section 31 is even more blunt: "No person shall carry on any work or undertaking that results in the harmful alteration, disruption or destruction of fish habitat."

DFO was also in a position to argue that society's values had changed vastly since 1950. What was acceptable then was not acceptable now. Every major industry in the country seemed to have acknowledged that, except Alcan. Even B.C. Hydro had, for the 1990s, adopted an enlightened environmental policy calling for the social and environmental impacts of all its power projects to be fully considered and, where possible, mitigated.

In August 1987, during the first week of the trial, after DFO scientists had presented evidence showing Alcan's low flow rates would be hazardous to salmon, an out-of-court settlement was suddenly reached. Closeted in a room under the guidance of UBC president Strangway, the Nechako River Working Group (NRWG) had, in just four days of secret talks, managed to break an impasse between Alcan and DFO that had existed for years. The group was made up of officials from DFO, Alcan, and the B.C. government. Going into the meeting, DFO had stripped from its team scientists like Alderdice and Hartman, who had been uncompromising in their fight to protect salmon. (The two men retired soon after, feeling abused and emotionally battered.) To further facilitate a deal, the group was given terms of reference that established the flow regime Alcan wanted. In other words, the group was told: "Here is the flow level Alcan wants and gets. Now make it work for the salmon too." According to DFO Pacific director Pat Chamut, the NRWG was not being told to reach a decision favourable to Alcan, but was simply "being challenged" to find a solution that worked for everyone.

Under the deal, Alcan gave up plans to dam the Nanika, but it kept control of the Nechako. The NRWG concluded chinook could be protected through a three-stage process. The first stage "should be sufficient" to conserve chinook, but if it failed, two back-up stages were proposed. The first stage called for cooling water releases from Kenney Dam, channel improvement work, sediment traps, fertilizing the upper river in spring, and fencing areas where cattle cause erosion. The second stage, to be implemented only after the first stage had been "demonstrated to be inadequate," would see artificial spawning dunes built in the river and clean gravel placed on spawning beds. The third stage would see construction of spawning channels, a hatchery, and compensation "in other systems."

As a last resort the NRWG stated that DFO should "maintain Nechako stock gene pool at some other hatchery." Each river system has its own unique gene stock that has evolved over eons. The NRWG, in recommending a sample be salvaged, was foreseeing the threatened extinction of Nechako River chinook.

In simple terms then, the deal was that DFO scientists and Alcan engineers would attempt to enhance the river on the one hand, while draining it of water on the other, despite a well-established biological tenet that increased flows are inexorably linked to increased stream productivity. And if it didn't work they would use the ultimate technological fix — a hatchery. If even that failed, they'd abandon the Nechako and try to make up for the loss of salmon by working on other rivers. It was a shocking compromise that jeopardized a valuable salmon run in order to ensure increased corporate profit.

Siddon accepted the proposal and wrote to Alcan to give his approval for Kemano Completion, stating: "I have received additional information which allows me to conclude that there exist alternative ways of providing an acceptable level of certainty for the protection of the fish."

Siddon and other top DFO officials said that under the deal, Kemano Completion and Nechako salmon would happily co-exist. That disregarded one big problem. In the years leading up to the court case, DFO scientists had thoroughly studied the

Nechako and had determined that Alcan's flow regime would be a disaster for the chinook that spawned in the upper reaches, and for the millions of sockeye that migrated through the lower river on their way to other systems. How to reconcile the contradiction? Siddon's way was to talk about "additional information," as if some new scientific breakthrough had taken place. In fact, the only additional information he had was the NRWG report — and that didn't offer any original research. Siddon and the NRWG had simply taken a leap of faith that a combination of approaches — some tested, some experimental — would yield positive results. They were rolling the dice with one of the most important salmon tributaries on the Fraser River system.

The federal government later tried to exempt Kemano Completion from mandatory public hearings under the environmental assessment review process (an EARP was ordered by the courts following a challenge by the Rivers Defence Coalition), saying it had already been studied to death. That was quite true — but the scientific studies had all concluded the project would devastate the salmon! The only positive reviews came from Alcan consultants and the NRWG, which acknowledged, and accepted, the possible destruction of the river.

≈

In the late 1980s, with the river running at about 70 percent of its natural level, chinook spawning escapements had slowly recovered, building up to about 1500 fish. That was far below pre-dam levels, but an improvement after the wipe-out of 1954-57 which saw stocks drop to 29 fish. Historical estimates for Nechako chinook stocks range from 5000 to 10,000 chinook, with one as high as 29,000. About 270,000 sockeye use the system, making it one of the most important salmon tributaries on the Fraser system, where, incidentally, the government announced in 1991 it would spend $100 million to double salmon stocks. If the Fraser salmon run is to be restored, it will have to be by maximizing the potential of key tributaries like the Nechako.

One of the startling things about the Nechako system is its immense potential for sockeye enhancement in connecting lakes. A technical DFO policy document, prepared in 1986 prior to the Alcan court challenge, states the lakes and rivers feeding into the Nechako could produce nearly 5 million sockeye. Another, earlier DFO document, "Toward A Fish Habitat Decision on the Kemano Completion Project," has even more impressive figures. It states the dominant cycle run to the Nechako (3.1 million sockeye) could grow to 31.7 million fish. It estimates current chinook production at 12,600 and sets the potential at 45,000. "The project threatens the fish habitats upon which these stocks depend," it warns. "The principal impacts stem from the major changes in the flow regimes."

Under natural conditions, the Nechako's flows would bottom out in February, and in March would begin a rapid increase, peaking in May and June. The high spring floods, among other things, flushed clean gravel beds and made the river ready for spawning. The flows dropped gradually through the summer, but remained high compared to what happened after the Kenney Dam was built. A graph of historic flows, compared to post-dam levels, shows the flow flattening dramatically from 1957 to 1979. Instead of rising and falling, the flow level undulates at around 200 cubic metres per second. Natural rates changed from about 50 centimetres in midwinter to over 400 centimetres in May. The profile for what happens to the river after Kemano Completion is like a flat line on a cardiogram, with one blip in July/August. There are no major flushing flows. And even during the "high" releases in midsummer, the Nechako does not reach the base low flow that scientists say is crucial.

So how will the Nechako spawning beds be cleaned now that nature has been stopped? Under the deal, mechanical cleansing

will be tried. It seems ludicrous that engineers believe they can
sweep up a river bottom as if it were a fish tank. But the positive
thinkers behind Kemano Completion say it's going to work.
They also plan to build spawning mounds because in the low
water imposed by Alcan, chinook will have to abandon many of
the places that nature had set aside for them. For reasons not
fully understood by humans, salmon choose certain areas in
streams to spawn. Each species has different preferences. Chinook like deep, fast-flowing, coarsely gravelled areas. The
minimum depth of water observed over chinook spawning beds
in the Nechako was 24 centimetres. At Alcan's rate of flow,
about 20 percent of the active redds would have water depths of
24 centimetres or less. The fish will either have to change their
genetic predispositions, or find somewhere else to spawn. That
somewhere else will have to be built for them.

Among the other problems presented by low flow levels are
these: in winter, incubating chinook eggs not adequately buried
under a thick blanket of water can freeze and die; even if they
don't freeze, ice can grind against the nests, crushing the delicate eggs; because of oxygen deprivation, the eggs can simply
suffocate. There is only one known engineering solution to those
dangers — the release of more water from the Alcan reservoir.
Such water releases are not called for, of course.

Low water creates problems in the summer too, when the
Nechako, which runs through the hard-baked Nechako Plateau
where there are only three to five days of rain in July, heats up
to levels that can be lethal to spawning fish.

"Severe reductions in flows may create points of difficult passage that block or delay migration of adult salmon. Flow
reductions can also cause river temperatures to rise to levels that
stress migrating salmon, resulting in delayed migration and
death without spawning. Delays not only concentrate fish, increasing the potential incidence of disease and loss through

predation, but also extend the migration period thereby decreasing energy reserves and reducing spawning success," states a DFO legal briefing paper.

Concern about delays in the Nechako, which runs into the Fraser River at Prince George, are serious because the sockeye salmon that migrate through the system to the Stuart River make extreme journeys that push them to the edge of their energy reserves. "A delay of more than five days will cause many of them to die without spawning," Alderdice and Hartman warned in a December 1990 article in the *Fisherman*, the newspaper of the United Fisherman and Allied Workers Union. "In addition to these threats to upper Fraser River sockeye and chinook salmon, another threat exists. A pulp mill may be built at Vanderhoof. The cumulative effects of all of these impacts will put the salmon runs of the whole upper Fraser River in jeopardy. Sockeye production, from the runs of the Nechako system, amounts to about one fifth of the total sockeye production for the whole Fraser system."

To address the problem of overheating, the NRWG agreed that Alcan would install a cold-water release device on the Kenney Dam — another experiment, and one which Alcan engineers had originally rejected when building the dam in the 1950s. In a 1954 article, R.W. Kraft, technical superintendent of Alcan's Kitimat works, said deep water releases weren't put in because they would have structurally compromised the dam. He also said it wouldn't help the sockeye anyway.

≅

Just downstream from Kenney Dam, spill-over water runs into the Nechako through Skins, Cheslatta and Murray lakes. The water roars down into the Nechako over Cheslatta Falls, plunging with brute force to the level of the river. Rainbows arc through the spray. The water hits the plunge pool with such force it surges back up in a standing wave 10 metres high. It is beautiful — and deadly. Nitrogen and oxygen are dissolved in the plunge pool, which is supersaturated with air bubbles. Gas bubbles may form in the blood and tissues of fish exposed to supersaturated solutions of nitrogen and oxygen. These bubbles block blood circulation, damage tissues and cause behavioural difficulties. The effects of total gas pressure (TGP) can be lethal. Alevins and fry are the most susceptible. Typically, bubbles will be seen in the dorsal fins of fish killed by TGP. When Alderdice studied the Nechako, he found the Cheslatta Falls were producing a phenomenally dangerous TGP problem. At 10 of 12 test stations below the falls he found chinook salmon could not survive. Alcan has agreed to tackle the problem by building a dam above Cheslatta Falls to release water under more controlled circumstances.

≅

In July 1986, DFO researchers D.W. Burt and J.H. Mundie completed "Case Histories of Regulated Stream Flow and Its Effects on Salmonid Populations." The report provided an extensive review of 81 case histories of regulated rivers, mainly in the Pacific Northwest. It found that in 76 percent, fish populations decreased. The cause of declines: reduced water flows. The study concluded the Nechako "has a 10 percent chance of maintaining the natural stocks."

States the report: "On this evidence it appears that the Kemano Completion Proposal carries a high risk for the affected salmonid populations."

It says that to avoid direct problems from reduced flow, "a guideline is that monthly flows should not be reduced below 30 percent of the natural regime." Under Kemano Completion the Nechako is to be reduced by 83 percent.

Addressing the plan to release cooling waters from Kenney Dam, the report raises the concern of chinook fry being stranded when the water levels rise, then drop. The study recounts an experiment on Campbell River to determine the effects of sudden flow reductions on young salmon. DFO researchers dropped the flow of the river from 110 centimetres to 34 centimetres. They got immediate and dramatic proof that small fish are unable to simply swim to deeper water when water levels decline. "The test had to be terminated prematurely to avoid mortalities of tens of thousands of chinook fry and yearling coho stranded or trapped in pools. Observations indicated that both species were reluctant to abandon their positions during falling water levels." The report said that "fluctuating flows disrupt spawning, cause stranding of juveniles, diminish food supply and scour spawning gravels." It also noted that such unnatural flows "can have a devastating effect on the total insect standing crop of a river" which is the main source of food for young fish. The flows, of course, will change dramatically under Alcan's control. The flushing freshets of spring will be gone, as will the gradual tailing off of the flow during the summer. Instead the river will be low in the spring, then will suddenly bump up for a few months in midsummer before dropping again. It will seem to the fish that the world has reversed itself. Gardeners might appreciate this analogy: imagine there is no rain all spring when the seeds are in the ground, then in summer there is sudden precipitation, accompanied by frosts.

The paper also warns that in releasing cooling water to ease the stress on migrating sockeye, Alcan "could create suboptimal temperatures for the growth of juvenile chinook salmon in the upper Nechako." At the top end of the river the water might be so cold it could stunt the growth of young chinook.

The 1984 DFO report "Toward A Fish Habitat Decision" concludes this way:

"The Nechako in its diminished state has already presented the Department with salmon habitat maintenance problems . . . the Department does not insist that the waters of all salmon rivers be reserved for the sole purpose of producing salmon, but it does adhere firmly to the more reasonable position of 'no net loss.' In other words, potential users of salmon waters must plan to avoid as many losses to salmon production as reasonably possible, and 'after the fact' they must stand ready to fully compensate for all damage. For the Department to require less would be to abandon its mandate which is to protect and preserve the fisheries resources of Canada.

"There is no perfect substitution for natural salmon habitat. If habitat is lost, the loss is likely to be irretrievable. One can partially compensate by producing salmon by alternative methods, but the substitution can only be regarded as second best: for one thing, in the case of hatchery production, the fish may not have the genetic characteristics of the wild stocks, and for another they are costly to produce. Moreover it is a cost that must be borne in perpetuity."

≈

From a fisheries management point of view the compromises made by DFO on the Nechako make no sense. A major salmon river, with great potential for enhancement, is being jeopardized while at the same time a fortune is being spent elsewhere on the Fraser system in an attempt to double salmon stocks. It doesn't make much sense from a societal viewpoint either, because aside from the short-term construction jobs, the economic benefits all go to a company using publicly owned water to generate power for private sale to the U.S. If Kemano Completion was a B.C. Hydro project, at least it could be argued the province was getting financial benefits from the destruction of the Nechako. So why did the deal happen? Simply because it's good for Alcan — and what's good for Alcan is good for the Conservatives.

Few companies are as close to Prime Minister Brian Mulroney as Alcan. The company has two directors who were made companions of the Order of Canada by Mulroney, two who were appointed Senators by him, one former ambassador who was a staunch supporter of Mulroney during the free trade campaign, and three who for years have served as advisers to Mulroney's administration.

David Culver, who retired as chairman and chief executive officer of Alcan in 1990, was named to the Order of Canada in 1988. Earlier that same year Culver led a pro-free trade lobby group, the Canadian Alliance for Trade and Job Opportunities, spending $2 million during the federal election to support the Tories. Alcan contributed $250,000.

In 1989, Alcan director Laurent Beaudoin was made a companion of the Order of Canada. Mulroney attended the reception. Two years earlier Beaudoin had been named to Ottawa's new defence industrial advisory committee. That same year he had spoken out publicly, extolling free trade and supporting Mulroney in Québec. In 1988 Mulroney named him to the Senate.

Alcan director Sonja Ingrid Bata (of the Bata shoe empire) was also a Mulroney supporter, and worked actively with Canadians for a Unifying Constitution, a group that tried to save the Meech Lake accord.

Allan Gotlieb, Alcan director, worked tirelessly promoting free trade when he was Canada's ambassador to the U.S. In 1989 he was named chairman of the Canada Council after a 25-year career in the federal public service and eight years in Washington. Gotlieb is a lobbyist who describes his work as "advising, strategizing for clients, looking at the political, legal, regulatory worlds."

Alcan director J.E. (Ted) Newall served on a group advising Mulroney on executive compensation in the public service and was also on the International Trade Advisory Committee.

The Honourable Jean-Marie Poitras, an Alcan director, was Michael Wilson's boss before Wilson became finance minister. Poitras was one of a group of Meech Lake loyalists named to the Senate by Mulroney in 1988.

Seeming like an odd man out on the board was Peter Pearse, a University of B.C. professor and a failed Liberal candidate who had emerged as a voice of reason in the environmental wars in B.C. In 1985 Pearse headed a task force that examined federal water policy. His group said huge water diversion projects, such as the proposed Grand Canal scheme in northern Québec, raised "profound environmental, economic and strategic questions." Pearse never publicly raised any profound environmental questions about Kemano Completion, however, and when I raised that point in a newspaper article he accused me of "slandering the Order of Canada" with my suggestion that Alcan had been given preferential treatment because of its connections.

It is possible Alcan's well-connected directors sat silently by while the Pacific arm of a rather minor ministry, DFO, moved to block Kemano Completion in the courts. It's possible the company never tried to use its political clout to get the government to back down from the rigid position it had taken, where its scientists argued Kemano Completion would destroy the river's valuable salmon run. It's also possible the Nechako salmon will live happily with the warm water and low flows DFO suddenly decided to accept, despite stacks of research papers that say the natural runs of the Nechako are doomed if the project goes ahead. It's all possible — but what will probably happen is that Alcan will get richer, and B.C.'s salmon resource will get poorer. On the Nechako River, the federal government has thrown away a great public resource to please a private corporation. It is justifying it by putting blind faith in the ability of technology to emulate nature.

≈

Walking across the riverbed of the Nechako below Kenney Dam, the dry sand and coarse gravel crunches underfoot. It must be my imagination, but the whole place seems to smell of salmon. There are none here. There haven't been any since

1954 when the river stopped flowing through the canyon above me.

I lie on the gravel under a spring sun, knowing chinook fry are emerging from redds in the river downstream, and dream of the Nechako passing over me, the water soft as silk. The river moves like great, shifting sheets of glass, reflecting green and gold light onto the riverbed. Salmon hold in the current like kites in the wind. Some of them have in their mouths the bones of the Cheslatta people, spilled from the coffins in the flood. I hear an osprey outside my dream, flying up the Nechako toward the dam. I realize it's right near here, just below Cheslatta Falls, that the federal government has set aside land for a hatchery. Just in case.

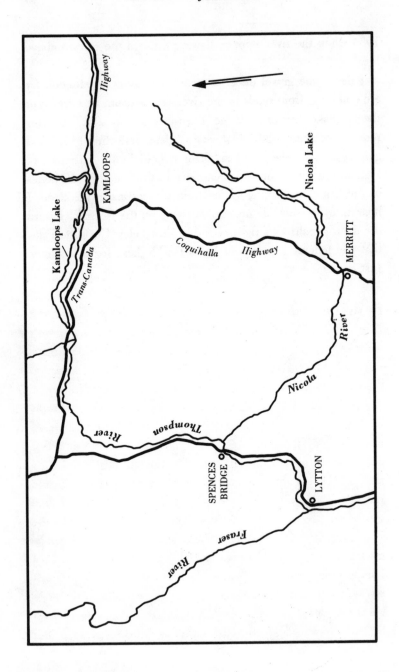

MOON IN ITS
HOUSE

The Thompson

By the time I'm knee deep, the bottom has disappeared in the river's murk. A few bends upstream, one of the Thompson's main tributaries, the Nicola, is in flood. Filled with mud from a logging operation near the Coquihalla Highway 50 kilometres to the southwest, the usually gentle Nicola is yawping at its banks. A river in such shape is said to have blown out. With trees removed by clearcutting, the litter on the forest floor torn up by the cross-yarding of downed timber, and the root network that holds the soil disintegrating, rainfall is sluicing off the hills. Instead of seeping into the groundwater, the rain gathers silt and runs straight into the Coldwater, north to the Nicola, and then west down the sun-baked Nicola Valley until it plugs into the Thompson River at Spences Bridge. When it finds me it wraps my legs in a swirl of water and dark brown brunosolic soil. Now I am wading blind, the aluminum cleats on my boots tapping out across the stones. On the walk to the river bank across table lands where the remains of ancient Indian villages are hidden beneath thickets and bunchgrass, the air smelled of sage. But waist deep in the insistent, tugging current of the Thompson, I smell earth, stratified rock, sandstone, shale, conglomerate and coal. Reminded that spawning fish find their natal streams by olfactory location, I put my hand in the cold water and feel the coarse burden of soil from the Cretaceous and early Tertiary periods sifting through my fingers. What does it smell like to the fish?

The river stretches out before me and seems to be tilting, moving like a mirror in a child's hand to catch the last light of the falling sun. I cannot see it from where I stand, but out there in the middle of the river the water is divided; the stained discharge from the Nicola hugs the south bank, but on the north side the Thompson runs clear. The river is silent except where it embraces my legs, murmuring secrets about glaciers.

I begin to cast, working out a heavy brown-and-gray fly with a blue tail called a Thompson River Rat. It is the size of a meadow mouse, and I cast with exaggerated slowness to allow the line to straighten behind me before I throw it forward. It falls on the water far out, and vanishes. It seems pointless to be fly fishing in these conditions, but you can't just stand and look at a river like this, not in October when the steelhead are returning from the sea, crossing five time zones and the International Dateline in their journey back from the North Pacific to a handful of streams braiding into the Thompson.

As I wade downstream, a black stallion comes to the river, regarding me as calmly as if I were a blue heron. After it drinks, taking long slow pulls that swell its belly with a bathtub full of water, three more horses materialize from a grove of poplars. Golden leaves shimmer in the breeze.

When the sun goes down I feel coldness in my hands, then in my knees and groin. I wade out to follow the horses back through the trees to the grassy fields beyond.

Does it matter if you catch a steelhead when you fish? To many it does not; it's enough to drink from the river.

≅

There was once a great glacier filling the Thompson and Nicola valleys, separated by a range of mountains with names that reflect their rugged history: Swakum, Gnawed and Glossy. The glacier linked the two valleys, forming a huge horseshoe of ice that pressed into the Interior Plateau where the subdued, rolling hills of the Intermontane Belt ride over a bed of volcanic and sedimentary strata. The remnants of that curving glacier, which was just one in a series, can be seen in Kamloops and Nicola lakes, long strings of blue water surrounded by blond bunchgrass and dry, green ponderosa pine. The terraces above the Thompson River were formed by centuries of erosion as the glacial melt raged to the sea. As the glacier retreated 10,000 years ago, steelhead nosed against the currents, searching for new homes.

Long regarded by some as a strain of rainbow trout that migrated to the sea, and seen by others as a true salmon, biologists since the mid-sixties engaged in a considerable taxonomic debate over steelhead. Finally, in 1989, the Names of Fishes Committee of the American Fisheries Society concluded there was no biological basis for distinguishing steelhead, or the broader rainbow trout family, from Pacific salmon. That did not mean steelhead weren't trout. It meant that although there were obvious differences in appearance and behaviour, all trout and salmon of a Pacific lineage were basically a single genus, or belonged to the same main family group. Biologists say steelhead salmon, but many people continue to use the old form of steelhead trout — and they are both right, in a way.

Steelhead will never be easy to classify. Behaviourally they are different from both rainbow trout and any of the five other species of salmon. Trout remain in fresh water lakes and rivers for their entire lives; steelhead go on long sojourns to the ocean. Salmon die after they spawn; steelhead do not have to, although many do. The picture becomes even more confusing when you consider that the offspring of rainbow trout and steelhead, when they occur together in a stream, will sometimes switch roles. That is, rainbow trout offspring can go to sea, becoming steelhead, and steelhead offspring can stay in fresh water, becoming trout. After four years, as adults, they will look profoundly different, even though they had common parents and emerged together from the same patch of gravel. The trout will have a thicker, rounder look, while the steelhead will be more slender, have a deeper silver sheen, and may be much larger. From the evidence, however, it seems the main thing that distinguishes steelhead from rainbow trout is a state of mind. Through DNA tracing, scientists may some day unravel the family tree of fishes and find out exactly where steelhead fit in, from which branch they first emerged. For me the answer is clear: they came off the glaciers millions of years ago, chunks of ice transformed into salmon.

For the most part steelhead are invisible. They migrate to the North Pacific, far out past the Aleutian Islands, rotating in a slow, anti-clockwise movement with the ocean currents to return, two or three years later, to the coastal streams of British Columbia, Alaska, Washington, Oregon and California. The Thompson run, which includes some of the biggest steelhead in the world, comes back around Vancouver Island to enter the mouth of the Fraser River at Vancouver. Along the way, thousands of them are intercepted by gillnet boats that are fishing for far more prolific runs of sockeye, chum, coho, pink and spring salmon. Coastwide, and at the Fraser specifically, steelhead run in such low numbers that, compared to salmon, they are classified as rare.

And they are getting rarer. The Thompson run is a case in point. There used to be 20,000 steelhead gathered in the pools and runs above and below Spences Bridge, but by 1990 stocks had fallen to only about 1500. In the spring of 1991, less than 1000 reached the spawning grounds. Biologists say 4000 spawners are needed to ensure the survival of the Thompson strain, an ecological subgroup that produces fish of exceptional size.

The Thompson steelhead return in September and October, coincident with runs of salmon that range into the millions. More than 90 percent of commercially intercepted steelhead are taken by gillnetters, most coming at key points in Georgia Strait and, late in the fall, within the lower reaches of the Fraser River itself, as the department of fisheries tries to harvest surplus salmon. Fishing in the south arm of the Fraser and in Georgia Strait immediately adjacent to the river, commercial fishermen take 1000 steelhead a season on average. In sub-area 29D, the main river from New Westminster to Mission, another 800 are landed. Many more steelhead are taken at sea. Biologists say that if a run of 10,000 Thompson steelhead turns in around Vancouver Island headed for the mouth of the Fraser, 8000 will be killed by nets before they reach the spawning grounds. It is abundantly clear that the glacier-born steelhead of the Thompson, the wild fish that carry a genetic make-up formed thousands of years ago, are facing extinction from an overharvest that is neither wanted, nor necessary. Gillnetting must be abandoned or radically altered as a method of fishing in Georgia Strait and the Fraser River. If it is not, Thompson steelhead will be eliminated.

Going up through the turbulent and murky waters of the Fraser, steelhead pass almost unnoticed. The 600 gillnet boats working the river will each see only an occasional steelhead, and the skippers on those boats will become angry and indignant if told they are helping to destroy a run of magnificent fish. In the fall of 1990 the federal government opened the Fraser fishery to harvest surplus chum. The salmon were considered surplus because they were above the levels needed on the spawning beds to replenish stocks. With one pulled in here, and another there, the gillnet boats took an estimated 600 Thompson steelhead in a 10-hour fishery designed to harvest 75,000 chum.

Don Reid, a commercial fisherman on the federal government's Fraser River Advisory Commission, defends the gillnetters, saying the Indian food fishery takes far more steelhead than the commercial fleet. Reid argues that gillnetters have already paid a high enough price by being forced to fish less and less on the Fraser.

"We've missed entire fall fisheries because of this Thompson steelhead problem," he complains. And he says gillnetters don't get enough credit for the efforts they make to release steelhead that aren't dead when pulled into the boat. He sums up the commercial fleet's steelhead conservation philosophy this way: "If it's still kicking, let it go."

Many fishermen, however, kill steelhead to eat themselves, or kill them because they are the cause of closure problems on the river. If the steelhead runs become extinct, they figure, they will get more time to fish for surplus salmon.

"One of the things that amazes me . . . is that there are some commercial fishermen who just want to fish these weak runs out, so we don't have to worry about them anymore," says Ken Malloway, chairman of the Interior Indian Fisheries Commission. Malloway acknowledges that steelhead runs are declining precipitously, but rejects any criticism of his group, saying native fishermen have voluntarily reduced fishing efforts to one day a week from three, in an effort to allow more Thompson fish to escape. "I think we put an extra 1500 fish on the spawning grounds last year," he says. Indian nets, however, are just as indiscriminate as nets set by commercial boats, and are often more effective per metre because they are strung in the current seams and niches that migrating fish favour. While the fishermen bicker, the fish slip towards extinction.

There can be no argument, however, that native food fisher-

men have a priority claim on fish in the Fraser system. Their ties
to the Thompson steelhead are rooted deep in history.

≈

Thompson River steelhead were first "discovered" in 1947
when Lee Straight, then outdoors editor of the Vancouver *Sun*,
heard a story from a classified ad salesman who had heard from
Carey Leachty, operator of the Big Horn Auto Court near
Spences Bridge, that a sports angler had caught some in the river.
Up until then it had been assumed steelhead couldn't get through
the wild waters in the lower reaches of the Fraser. Straight, being
a good journalist, went up to investigate the rumours for himself.
That fall he found the river full of steelhead.

"You could go across on a cable car here and see fish lying all
across the river," he recalled one day as we talked on the riverbank at Spences Bridge. "I caught some, wrote about it, and
we've never looked back. It's very badly depleted now, obviously.
It was easy to catch steelhead then . . . I would guess the run is
25 percent to 10 percent of their past levels."

In 40 years, the Thompson run has been reduced by up to 90
percent.

The steelhead were in the river for an eon before sportsmen
found them in 1947. The Thompson Indians knew about them,
although they did not know they were steelhead and could never
have dreamed of the great ocean voyages the fish had taken.

Within a few kilometres of where the Nicola pours into the
Thompson, archaeologists have recorded 19 separate village
sites. Many more are located downstream to the confluence with
the Fraser and upstream to where the main river emerges from
Kamloops Lake. Typically, you will find pit houses built on river
terraces overlooking prime fishing runs. Just up the Nicola Valley, Indian graves are found on talus slopes above the river.

Prior to 1858, when white influence became strong in the region, the Thompson Indians had a dynamic culture that was

intricately interwoven with the natural world. They understood
the wind when it sang and could hear the secrets whispered by
the river. They fished for steelhead in the winter using spears
and pitch lamps (they still do at times), and treated the big fish
with a special reverence. When James Teit went into the area in
1895, collecting information for the American Museum of Natural History, he recorded practices that revealed the respect
natives had for steelhead.

The Thompson Indians had fantastic, elaborately evolved artistic practices. They covered their faces and bodies with complex,
abstract symbolism — paintings and tattoos that graphically repre-
sented the planets, sorrow, fear, the weeping earth, reflections in
a lake, crossing clouds. Before white contact, which quickly led to
abandonment of the behaviour, everyone had their faces painted
on an almost daily basis to reflect dreams or project power.

One day a noted hunter called Tsa'la had a bad dream about
grizzly bears, so he painted a red circle around his face to ward
off the danger portended in the dream.

A young woman etched a crude outline of a man on her body,
for luck in finding her future husband; another favoured a five-
pointed mountain flower as a love charm.

A man who had an earth spirit for a guardian painted a blue
streak over each eyebrow (clouds on the horizon); the right half
of his chin was red and the left, blue (a mystery lake with two
colours of water); a large triangle in red pointing towards his nos-
tril covered the left cheek (representing a mountain with trees);
on his right cheek were four vertical red and yellow lines extending to the lower jaw (the tears of the earth). So painted, he was a
man who had become the earth.

One small but striking symbol used in tattoos showed a circle
within a circle crossed by a line. It looks just like a fish eye, but
is called "moon in its house."

Amidst these brilliantly daubed faces with bars, triangles and circles of red, yellow, blue and white, glistening with powdered micaceous hematite, there appeared at special times people whose faces were a sombre, solid black. Teit, who got most of his information from a shaman named Baptiste Ululame'llst, or Iron Stone, said warriors gained the right to paint their faces black only when they had killed an enemy. Hunters, when they killed a bear of any kind, also blackened their faces as a mark of respect and token of death. "It put the bear in the same category with human beings," said Teit.

About the only other time men painted themselves black was when they went to the river to spear the "huge trout" that collected there in the winter, and which miraculously rose from the depths to inspect their flickering pitch torches. Those trout, far too large to be river residents, were really steelhead, the rarest and most beautiful of the six salmon species. Face painting has vanished, but the fish remain, and they still inspire rituals among those who seek them.

≅

It is a bright fall day. A sharp wind scuds down the valley, rattles through a grove of tall cottonwoods, banks off the dry hills where wild horses roam the coulees, and drives tumbleweeds down the dirt roads. Above the gentle murmur of the river I can hear fly fishermen coming. They wade noisily through the shallows and crunch across the gravel bars just upstream from the old crossing at Spences Bridge. A dusty parking lot fills with pickups. The fishermen come wearing sleeveless vests that bulge with pockets full of leaders, extra lines, fly boxes, spare reels and more than the occasional flask of whiskey. Bright flies bristle from hat brims and breast patches of sheep's wool. They carry slender rods that are up to 12 feet long, and wear chest waders, wide brimmed hats or baseball caps to shield their eyes from the sun, and polarizing glasses to cut the water's glare. Under the trees, standing next to a waist-high cairn covered with plastic wrapping, the president of the Steelhead Society of British Columbia waits patiently, pondering what he is about to say.

Ehor Boyanowsky, a tall, graying university professor, heads a small organization of about 800 steelheaders. Many of them are on the Thompson this late October afternoon not just to fish, but also to pay homage to one of their members. The cairn, made from river stones taken from the Thompson's bed, is to commemorate the late Cal Woods, one of the society's most respected members. As secretary of the group, he tirelessly fought for the protection of steelhead rivers in the province, writing uncounted letters to government leaders, industrialists, newspaper editors and anybody else who would listen. In the process he gave the society a louder voice than its small numbers warranted. He kept writing, even when he was dying of cancer.

"No river was more dear to him than the Thompson. No fish were more loved by him than Thompson steelhead," says Boyanowsky. "Cal's spirit rests in the hearts of those who loved him, and in the river and in the steelhead that he so loved." He unveils the cairn and in a momentary silence that follows I hear a deep, distant ripping sound as a big fish breaks the surface.

As a criminology professor at Simon Fraser University, Boyanowsky studies with calm detachment the evils of humanity. He comments with academic interest on the motivations of sociopathic criminals. But when he turns to the subject of the killing of Thompson steelhead by the commercial gillnet fleet, emotion rises in his voice. "It's unbelievable. The natives are cutting back. The sports fishermen are cutting back, but the commercial fishery continues to decimate the runs!

"Thompson River steelhead have been commercially intercepted to the brink of extinction. It is appalling!"

Boyanowsky takes the fall semester off each year so that he can be on the river. I found him in a dilapidated fruit picker's cabin he had rented near the Hilltop Gardens fruit stand, just northeast of Spences Bridge on the Trans-Canada Highway. The Waterboys blast from a portable cassette player while he ties flies at the kitchen table. The driving, moody vocals of "Fisherman's Blues" fill the room: "I wish I was a fisherman/Tumblin' on the seas/Far away from dry land/And its bitter memories." On one wall of the sparsely furnished cabin is a Ken Kirkby portrait of a steelhead; on another, a plan of the river drawn by an architect, with all the key steelhead lies marked as precisely as if they were supporting beams in a skyscraper. Steelhead like to rest in the same locations year after year, so a fly fisherman who spends a lot of time on a river accumulates knowledge over the seasons, mapping out the holding waters. One who knows a river can fish it quickly, bypassing vast stretches of unproductive water and searching out the almost invisible fish in the grooves they have found amid the green boulders on the river bed. Even so, Boyanowsky will make thousands of casts for every steelhead he takes. "I'll raise three fish a day, on average, and take one of them," he says as he wades waist deep in the cold waters of the river. The greasy boulders on the bottom shift under his feet, and he walks at times with his arms out, balancing between two worlds. The algae that coats the rocks, making them so treacherous to wading anglers, is a sign of the river's fecundity. The Thompson is an extremely rich environment compared to the relatively sterile coastal rivers. But while the river's plentiful food supply helps young steelhead grow, it is not the Thompson's protein resource that explains the remarkable size the adult fish attain.

≅

Among those I met at the Cal Woods memorial was Henry Tsuyuki, a retired fisheries scientist who has been fascinated by the Thompson fish since 1957, when he first began to study them.

Tsuyuki says Thompson steelhead are a unique strain, molded
by the glaciated landscape and the tumultuous waters. On average they are bigger than almost any other strain of steelhead in
the world, with the only real rivals coming from the brawling
Skeena system in northwestern B.C.

Tsuyuki, a soft-spoken man whose eyes sparkle when he's talking about steelhead, says the Fraser River canyon played a key
role in shaping the genetic make-up of the Thompson fish. Now
broached by fish ladders, the canyon was once a "murderously
difficult piece of water" for migrating fish. Studying steelhead
strains, Tsuyuki found that the Thompson fish, and those that
run farther up the Fraser to the Chilcotin River, have unique
traits. "What we have today is from 10,000 years ago," he says,
nodding out towards the river where steelhead lie unseen. "What
makes the Thompson fish special, aside from their extraordinary
size, is their very strong ability to swim. They are powerful fish.
They leap out of the water a lot when they are hooked. It's quite
a unique resource." When he first came to the river the fishing
was tremendous. "I'd like to see it that good again, but I'm not
sure I ever will," he says sadly.

Tsuyuki said one of the changes he's seen on the Thompson
over the years is a persistent drop in water levels. "We used to
fish it in the fifties and the water was always three or four feet
higher," he said, noting the broad, exposed gravel beds nearby.
"Once you get logging the land won't hold the water; it comes
off all at once." When the Nicola and other tributaries aren't getting blown out by logging run-off, they are being drawn down by
agricultural use.

Under B.C. law, fish have no legal rights to water. There is no
base flow reserved for them. Ranchers, farmers and industries lease
water rights, and they can pump rivers into their factories and
onto their fields, even through summer drought when the bones

of the riverbed jut out and the pools become tepid traps for young fish.

Also troubling is the presence of dioxins in the Thompson, and in the flesh of resident rainbow trout caught below Kamloops, where a pulp mill discharges effluent into the river. Fishermen in the small resource town, where the stink of sulphur hangs in the air like L.A. smog, have been advised to stop consuming downstream trout. It is known that salmon fry in the Fraser have been contaminated by dioxins as well, and there is little doubt that steelhead, which spend two or three years in freshwater, are capable of picking up the tremendously potent toxin. A spectrum of other pollutants, discharged in low levels but vast amounts, are released along with the dioxins — resin and fatty acids, chlorinated phenols and other substances. The full environmental impact of pulp mill effluent is not understood, but it is known to affect the productivity rates of fish and aquatic insects, to reduce disease resistance and to change behavioural traits. The sublethal response of trout exposed to pulp mill effluent is often so extreme that a fish loses its equilibrium or becomes immobilized. Scientists call it "functional death."

"It's what you can't see that has devastating effect," says Tsuyuki. "If you use the resource intelligently there's no reason it should disappear. But I worry about the Thompson River. I hope the steelhead will be able to survive."

Like some of the others gathered on the river bank that day, Tsuyuki said he didn't fish much anymore. But he liked to come to the river anyway, to be close to the steelhead, and to the fishermen.

While we talked a young man, wild eyed from lack of sleep, his hair blown by the wind, told of the fish he'd taken that morning. Bright as chrome, sixteen pounds and running like a freight train. Word was spreading with a whisper through the crowd that a steelhead, caught and released that very morning by a bait fisherman, had weighed almost 40 pounds, close to a world record 42-pound fish that had been netted in the Skeena.

Since 1987 sports anglers have been required to let all wild Thompson steelhead go; weights are calculated on the basis of length and girth. Many Thompson fishermen started catch-and-release long before the law required them to.

≅

Ken Kirkby, a Toronto artist who fishes with a delicate fly rod and a trance-like look on his face, first fished the Thompson in 1958. He was on his way to fish somewhere else when nightfall caught him at Spences Bridge. He stopped for the evening and heard about big trout in the river. The next day he caught a 5-pound resident rainbow. Then he heard about the steelhead. He never made it to the lake he was headed to that year, and has been back on the Thompson most falls since. He dreams about it and, like a steelhead, knows its scent.

"Eventually I equated the odor of this river, beyond the sage and beyond the dry soil, to a smell of trout and steelhead."

Kirkby, 50, spent several years in the Arctic as a young man, travelling with an Inuit family. He became entranced by Inukshuks, the stone figures that dot the barren northern landscape, guiding hunters to prey and leading them home again. He paints the stone men almost exclusively now, a passion that has led him out of artistic oblivion into the light of mainstream acceptance. It seems that once he had seen an Inukshuk, he didn't really have any choice about it. "When I first saw one I knew I'd found something so powerful it would've made Goya's skin creep."

Kirkby embraces obsession, as do most fly fishers, and it doesn't take much to get him to tell the story of his first Thompson steelhead. Returning to the big river in 1959 he didn't know where to find the fish. There was no architectural plan, no map inside his head. So he began his journey with a methodical upriver dissection of the current, covering as much water as he could. He would cast and retrieve, take a few paces and repeat the process. It's called fishing blind.

Standing in the Log Cabin Inn, his eyes blazing and a beer sloshing dangerously close to the lip of the mug, he recalled groping up the Thompson. There were no Inukshuks to guide him, but he sensed he was being led somewhere. "I walked my way, obsessively, stone by stone, up the river. I made a cast to the shallow end of a pool. I saw a fish, its head and shoulders coming out of the water behind the fly. I didn't want to strike. I was afraid I'd miss it. Then I struck and the fish tail-walked across the water. Wow. That experience got me totally bonded to this river.

"This fish, it was probably about 15 pounds, I don't know, everything about it, the difficulty of getting it, the way it fought, the way it looked — it seemed it was legendary. I put it back in the water." He had always killed his fish before, but catching steelhead can change things.

≅

There are only a handful of streets in the wind-blown truck stop town of Spences Bridge, which lies pinched between the Trans-Canada Highway and the Thompson River. One street is called Steelhead, and if you walk down it and go straight into the river you won't be in a bad place. The highway was once the biggest thing in the world to Spences Bridge, but people are beginning to realize that, in the long run, it's the river at their backs that's important. There are four gas stations in town, but two have closed since a new highway, the Coquihalla, opened to the southwest, siphoning off traffic by providing a more direct link between Vancouver and Kamloops. A motel on the Trans-Canada at Spences Bridge is a reminder of what happens when traffic deserts a highway town. It has a swimming pool full of tumbleweed, a boarded-up restaurant and a sign that hangs down on one end, swinging in the wind. On fall weekends the only people stopping there are steelheaders, overflow from the two motels along the river.

Steelhead have been important to the local economy since sportsmen found the fish in the late 1950s. Even though angler days have dropped off from a high of 15,000 to 8000 a year because of reduced steelhead runs, fishing keeps Spences Bridge alive for part of the year.

"Without the steelhead fishing in the fall this town would dry up. From the last week of September until the end of December it's the only thing going on here. It's all we've got," says John Stepp, who runs the Log Cabin Inn, a bar where anglers and local ranchers gather in the evenings.

Just up the street, on North Frontage Road, Burrell and Emma's coffee shop bustles in the early morning with a steady stream of fishermen. Burrell and Emma both have pacemakers now, and are often away in the southern U.S., but fishermen get a warm greeting anyway as they elbow up to the counter to order steak and eggs, or stacks of pancakes. A few blocks away the steelhead lie as still as ice in the river. They do not eat after they enter the river in September, and will fast until after they have spawned in small tributaries in April. It isn't known why they don't feed, but they come in layered with fat, ready for a long wait. Perhaps the biggest mystery is why these fasting fish will rise from the bottom to take a garishly coloured fly, fished so that it rakes across the surface in a fast-moving arc. But rise they do, coming up from the green depths to roll out and take the offering in a slow, powerful manner. Steelheaders learn not to strike immediately, as they do with trout or other salmon, but to let the steelhead have its way, to hold the fly and sink from sight. Then the rod is swung off to the downstream side with a quick, smooth movement. If it is done right, the fly lodges in the back corner of the steelhead's mouth, a barbless hook piercing tough cartilage. It is thought that steelhead take a fly out of sheer aggression, or because they are reacting instinctively. Perhaps it is because they are bored, lying there on the bottom of the river, or perhaps it is because the flies are as beautiful and alive as pitch lamps and it is just the right thing to do. At any rate, they don't seem to have much choice about it. When it happens, it's a natural and wild event.

≅

Shortly before 5 p.m., the moon rose in its house over a ridge to the south of the river and that is when the steelhead took my fly. The line was drifting, lost in the dark shimmering water, when the steelhead plucked the Green Butt Skunk from the surface and turned, towards the moon. It made the movement so quickly the hook was driven into the upper right corner of its mouth. The fish was running before I really knew what was happening, and then it jumped so far away, so high, that it seemed not to be connected to me. The line was heavy. It arced into the river and came out showering a fine spray when it was pulled tight. The steelhead went across the river like a freight train, and Ehor Boyanowsky waded down with my fishing partner, Nick Didlick, to tell me to follow. Kirkby was just below, reeling in his line, shouting out joyfully every time the fish jumped. Numb, stumbling over the rocks, watching the line vanish from my reel, I wished I had painted my face black before I came to the river that evening. Boyanowsky put his hand out to steady me. "Keep the rod to the side," he said. "Don't give her an excuse to go downstream or you'll never see her again."

After 15 minutes I began to ache. This is where a big steelhead gets you, begins to wear you down: in the forearm and biceps, in the wrist and, of course, in the heart. "The river is against me, this will never work," I thought. But finally it came in and it was a female, 18 pounds, as silver and as perfect as the moon, with pink blush on the cheeks and black spots splattered across a green back. I held the fish among the speckled stones, pulled out the fly.

The history of the ocean and the river and the earth is written on the skin of steelhead, etched in the scales. I pushed her back into the river so she could tell her story to the glaciers.

SWIMMING
AT NIGHT

The Deadman

The last exit before the oblivion of Kamloops Lake is the
Deadman River, where steelhead hang an abrupt left and disappear. Months earlier they were gliding over the Emperor Sea
Mounts off the northeastern coast of Russia. But turning out of
the powerful, clear Thompson River, with the blue waters of
Kamloops Lake in sight above them, the big fish head up a
small, dirty stream to begin the last stage of their journey. They
started here four or five years ago and have been searching for
the scent of the Deadman since they entered the mouth of the
Fraser in the fall. It must smell to them of topsoil, volcanic rock,
rotting trees, shaded cottonwoods and jackpine, of deer bones,
alfalfa, diesel and the stink of cattle.

The Deadman is a troubled river that rushes through subsis-
tence ranchland where 'for sale' signs mark the retreats of men
from their dreams. Perhaps it is the unforgiving, hardbaked
earth that has defeated them, leaving their barns and houses to
slump like exhausted drunks and their fences to stagger and
pitch to the ground. Or maybe it is the five hoodoos that stand

on a steep mountainside over the river, so hidden in the timber you can only see them when the light is just right. For some the bad luck runs deep. Crops wither in the summer heat; spring floods erode the narrow strip of bottom land. One rancher stopped to open a gate and was run over by his own truck, whose emergency brake had failed. Now the widow is selling out, but the river isn't waiting for a dignified departure; it has cut sharply into her farmyard, undermining the barn and outsheds, tugging at their foundations, trying to suck them into the current, to blow them out down the valley, to spread the planks from the barn through a thousand log jams and carry the remaining pieces into the big river and on to the great sea.

The Deadman got its name after Pierre Charette, clerk of the North West Trading Company at Kamloops, was killed here in 1817 in what has been reported, rather unsatisfactorily, as a quarrel over the choice of a campsite. Imagine, if you will, the number of places a man could have found to camp in this empty land in 1817. Did people really kill each other over such things? Perhaps they did in the 1800s, when every brook, every murmuring, shining stream seemed to promise gold. The Deadman promised, sparking a rush in the 1860s, but it didn't deliver much until 1930 when a "big play" was found in the upper valley at Vidette Lake. That led to one mine, but the Deadman was no new Klondike. The big play played out, leaving rocky soil that was too poor for farming and natural meadows where the waving grass enticed ranchers with whispers of prosperity.

The Deadman River drains a quadrant of the Fraser Plateau, rising in a series of lakes, running due west then turning abruptly south and winding its way to the Thompson. Along the way it plunges over a fall of 170 feet (which cuts steelhead off from the upper river) and enters a great chasm that is 700 feet deep and from one to two miles wide. Where the chasm opens along the river, the flat land offers the greatest agricultural poten-

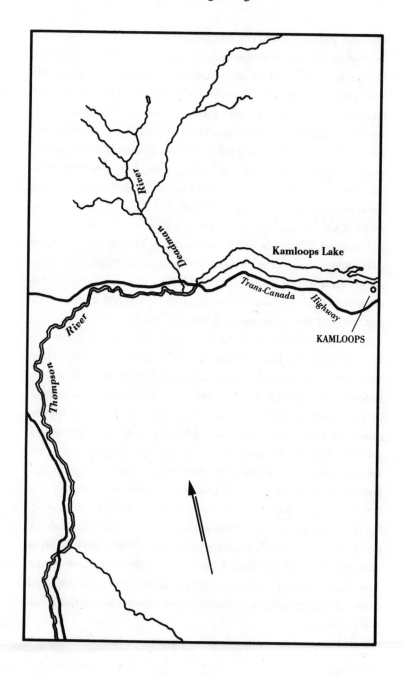

tial. Ranchers settled where the natural meadows once stood and soon were hard at work clearing more land. In 1919 the British Columbia department of lands surveyed the area and concluded that, although the soil and climate wouldn't permit profitable farming, cattle ranchers could make a go of it. "The chief assets are the abundance of summer feed and good water. Stock do well. All we saw were in good condition and most of the cattle were rolling fat," reported the land agents. They noted plentiful mule deer, grouse and rabbits, but made no mention of any fisheries value in what was originally called Riviere des Defunts, or River of the Dead.

Deadman Chasm is a dry land that has broken the hopes of gold seekers and begrudgingly grants a living to those who struggle to ranch it. Despite the hardships, there is magic between the steep hills, and you sense it soon after turning off Highway 97 just west of the sawmill town of Savona.

≈

Ian McGregor's B.C. Ministry of the Environment pickup truck rattles off the end of pavement onto the dirt of the Deadman River road. It is mid May and the alfalfa fields along the bottom land are lush, fading to lighter shades of green where the bunch-grass and pine forest from the highlands merge at the base of precipitous slopes. He looks on the agrarian landscape without any fondness. His eyes are following the river bank as it twists back and forth across the narrow valley like a deer running in panic.

"We spent $35,000 on that corner right there," he says, slowing the truck as we near an inward curve of the river, here about two lanes wide and fast with spring melt. The corner is piled deep with rip-rap, a jumble of boulders fronting a berm of mixed stone and gravel. The current churns at the bank, deflecting in whorls and back eddies. Inside the protective berm are the fields of a small ranch.

"This guy says he loses five or ten acres a year to the river.

He fights against it. He's in there all the time with his Cat, but you can see how it's eaten away at his land farther down. The berm is working, but you wonder how much more would have to be spent to protect his whole place. At what point, you have to ask, are you spending more to save the land than the ranch is worth?"

Farther upstream, passing onto an Indian reserve, McGregor points out where native workers have cabled hundreds of pine trees to the bank, the trunks lashed down, the tree tops waving in the current.

"This is a new technique and it seems to be working really well. The tree branches soften the current, protecting the bank from erosion, and it gives young fish good hiding places. There is lots of shade and cover there. But it's hard work. Last spring about 50 percent of the trees washed away in a flood and they all had to be replaced."

Higher up, softened by Skookum, Snowhoosh and Mowish lakes, and still shaded by vegetation, the Deadman is a gentler river. In places it comes through the forest like a Haydn concerto, with the notes drifting in the deeper pools, spilling through the riffles and dancing down long, smooth runs. Where ranchers have stripped away the streambank cover, however, there is no symphonic proportion to it; the river runs fast, slashing at its banks, trying to cut away the corners so it can go straight to the Thompson.

"This is our biggest problem," says McGregor, stopping his truck to look out on a ranch that boasts alfalfa fields that sweep right down into the river. "The early ranchers tried to take out every bloody tree. Every cottonwood they could find they cut down. They devegetated the river. And they have done everything they can to straighten it out, to take out the bends. Ranchers like a river that runs straight. But when you take the curves out, you speed it up and it only causes you more problems. The river is highly volatile now."

The cattle that wander through the grazing pastures are continuing the devegetation. They eat everything in sight. They lumber along the streambanks, chewing at every willow bush, every young cottonwood that takes root, turning the streambank vegetation into cud and green saliva. They trample pathways to the stream, creating muddy wallows. The result: unstable banks that wash away when the water runs high in the spring. You can see it now from up on the roadway; the water is the colour of dark loam. Flood and erosion haunt the ranchers but it is hard to be sympathetic for, to a large degree, they are simply being revisited by the sins of the past.

"It is better now than it once was," says McGregor, trying to find reason for hope. "But it's nothing like it should be. It's nothing like it was historically. You can go to the upper valley and see the Deadman in its natural state with lots of vegetation on the banks. It's a pretty sight."

≅

McGregor first came to Deadman Chasm in 1977, the year after he was named biologist in charge of saving the Thompson River steelhead run. When he started, virtually nothing was known about the big fish that came up the Thompson except that an extraordinary sports fishery had developed at Spences Bridge. Nobody knew how many fish there were, but everyone said there were an awful lot less than there used to be. The sports fishery by then was about 20 years old, and by today's standards it was still excellent. But it wasn't what it had been. So McGregor started to put the puzzle together: How many fish were there? How many should there be? What did they need to survive and flourish?

Just about the first thing he did was to radio-tag a batch of steelhead. He wanted to know where they went after they left Spences Bridge. A few weeks later he found himself heading north up the Thompson in his pickup, past Ashcroft, then west, staying with the mainstem past Walhachin and on towards Kam-loops Lake. Above the lake the main river branches into the North and South Thompson, and there is a lot of good water up there for steelhead. He thought that was where the steelhead were taking him. Historically there are references to steelhead as far up the North Thompson as Barrier Creek, 70 kilometres northeast, but biologists now believe those were big rainbow trout from Kamloops Lake, misidentified as steelhead. In 14 years of radio tracking, not a single steelhead has ever been known to pass through Kamloops Lake. Deadman is the last stop for Thompson steelhead.

McGregor was surprised when he found his truck turning north off Highway 97, heading up the narrow Deadman, honing in on the sharp "pip, pip, pip" of radio signals. The quartz crystals in the transmitters gave each fish its own unique frequency. Running across the dial on the radio receiver, McGregor realized the whole school of transmitting fish was turning up the Dead-man. When the road came down next to the river he stopped his truck, and walked the bank. Wearing polaroid glasses to cut through the surface glare, it wasn't long before he found his first steelhead, a greenbacked fish hovering over a gravel mound, ghostlike at the tail of a pool. In heavily silted water it is hard to make out fish. You have to know where to look and you have to look hard. You key on shapes, colour tones and movement. What McGregor could see was really no more than a gray shadow vanishing and briefly reappearing as the current shifted veils of silt near an oval of gravel that had been cleaned by the repeated brushing of a fish's tail. Even so, he was elated. He had just un-covered one of the great secrets of the Thompson River steelhead. He had found their birthplace. It was a secret they had kept for 10,000 years before the arrival of Europeans, and for 200 years after prospectors and settlers moved in.

"It's amazing," said McGregor, "to think that for all those

years these huge fish were coming here to spawn and none of
the ranchers here knew anything about them. They slipped in
when the river was cloudy with run-off and were gone before
anybody knew they were here."

It is little wonder nobody knew about the steelhead. They
spawn during a brief period from mid-April to the end of May
when the river is silted and running so heavily that nobody
thinks of fishing it. They come in when the people of the chasm
are distracted with flood problems, calving, and seed crops. And
just to make sure the secret is kept, the steelhead hold to cover
during the day. They move upstream through the open riffles
where their backs might show only after darkness falls. They
swim at night in the River of the Dead.

≈

Biologist Alan Caverly pulls green waders up to his chest, lifts
back two large plywood trapdoors, and vaults down into the
swirling current of the Deadman. He is waist deep in a small pen
that is barred on three sides. The river churns through the bars
and boils around his waist. The fourth wall of the cell, downstream, is notched with a V-shaped opening less than a foot wide.
Stretching across the stream is a fence that blocks any upstream
movement of fish. When steelhead encounter the Deadman fish
trap, set beneath a dramatic, rainbow-hued, volcanic cliff, they
nudge back and forth along it until the V-gate leads them into
the holding pen. The largest number of steelhead to pass
through the fence in a single year was 1200. That was in 1984,
when runs peaked. They have been on a downward trend ever
since. Total this year, with only a few days left in the season:
144. The Deadman steelhead are falling towards extinction.

It is early afternoon. Caverly has held some steelhead for me
from the night before. Some years there have been as many as
100 steelhead a night pushing their way into the trap. Last night
was typical for this year: three. They are stored in long black

plastic tubes that undulate in the current. The fish are calm; it is as if they know they are going to be released unharmed. Unzipping a tube slowly, Caverly points the open end towards a dip net. In a sudden explosion a steelhead appears from the blackness, surging out of the current and into the net. The fish is silver and green, with a heavily spotted back and a bold pink stripe riding down its side from cheek to tail. The stripe looks like the tail of an Amazon parrot — brilliant and wild. The fish is as long as a man's leg. The average weight of Deadman steelhead is 12 to 14 pounds. This one is about 12 pounds.

Caverly wears a woolen glove on his left hand, so he can get a better grip on the fish. He reaches down into the water, his arm disappearing up to the elbow. His face is so close to the river he can feel the cold air above the surface. "This is a very wet job," he says. "You get used to being soaked day after day." He is searching for the part of the fish that narrows before it flares into a broad, translucent tail. That place is called the wrist. On a 12-pound fish, the wrist is just about the thickness of a human wrist. It is firm muscle. The fish is as cold as ice and as smooth as a peeled mango. Without a glove, Caverly's hand would slip on the steelhead's protective coating. Most people call the mucous covering "slime," thinking of the clammy, viscous substance that covers a dead fish at the market. But on a healthy wild steelhead, "slime" is beautiful and functional. The slick, glistening lubricant lets a fish slide through the grit and friction of the current and protects it from bacterial infection.

Caverly gropes in the water like a blind man for a moment, his right hand sliding up the steelhead's belly to rest behind its steel gray head, the plates of the gills gasping with excitement just in front of his fingers. His left hand fixes on the wrist. Then he stops moving and smiles. "Okay," he says and lifts the steelhead. It emerges from the dark water as if by magic; it is an astonishing sight. A brilliantly lit, vibrant steelhead, its mouth slightly agape, its eyes showing alarm, its body rigid. He is holding in his hands a million years of genetic selection — a fish the size of a small child. The colours seem to be neon against the dullness of the river. I look around at Deadman Chasm, at the dry land, the sad ranches and the cliff called Split Rock. I think: this surely is one of nature's great wonders.

Biologists have come to realize that every salmon stream has its own unique genetic coding. Steelhead from the Deadman are biologically identical to steelhead from other systems in B.C., but at the same time they are different. Each stream has a stock that has evolved over thousands of years to perfectly fit its environment. With individual stocks of wild salmon vanishing rapidly throughout the Pacific Northwest, largely because of habitat alterations, fisheries biologists have realized with a sense of urgency that every small brook that produces fish is vital. If the Deadman stock is eliminated it can never be replaced and it will dramatically weaken the larger Thompson run, of which it historically made up about 30 percent. (The remainder of the run comes largely from the Coldwater and Bonaparte rivers, which are in marginally better shape than the Deadman.) Steelhead populations in the Thompson system have fluctuated up and down over the decades, but began a disturbing downward trend in 1985. By 1991 the overall Thompson population had fallen to under 1000. The system historically had runs of about 20,000 fish. The Deadman, which should be supporting 3000 steelhead, instead has less than 150. If the unique Deadman strain falls below 50 fish, it may have hit a point of no return, after which extinction is highly probable.

"We have reached the point where we need every fish back. We just can't afford to lose a single one," McGregor has told me. "We are starting to talk about an endangered species here."

Sean Dunn, a 16-year-old student on the resource management program at NorKam Secondary School, takes the net handle from Caverly and gingerly lifts the fish from the trap. He wades upstream from the fence, then bends down, catches the steelhead by the wrist and pulls it from the dipnet. He holds it, nose into the current. After a few minutes the fish struggles, its strength coming back. Dunn opens his hand and the steelhead vanishes. Chad Arden, 17, another student working at the counting fence, takes a second fish from Caverly. A stocky kid who looks like he could create mayhem in a loose ruck, Arden cradles the big steelhead as gently as if it were a baby. Sports anglers treat wild fish in the same way, and studies have shown more than 99 percent survive release. Arden smiles when he feels the fish kicking for freedom. "There you go," he says, pushing it tenderly into the river. I have to wonder if his kids will ever have the chance to experience that.

Walking up above the fence, Caverly peers into the murky current. "There was a pair spawning just up here the other day," he says smiling happily. We see a broad, dark tail the size of a dinner plate swirl near the surface, then disappear. "There!" he says. The fish surfaces again. "Oh no, it's not a spawner. It's a kelt. A male that's already spawned, and he's in rough shape." We can see white patches on his head and flanks where bacterial pathogens have invaded the body, attacking in openings where the slime has been worn away. He does not glisten like the fish just released. The shocking pink stripe he once wore has faded to a rust stain.

"We've had as many as 10 percent of the steelhead here come back as repeat spawners, but all of them have been females so far," says Caverly, watching the fish struggle in the current. "The males have a rough time. They stay in the stream longer. They wait for the last female to show up, and they fight a lot. They come in first, leave last — and for most of them it is just too much. I don't think that one will make it."

The fish fence will be gone in a few weeks, and when most of the steelhead stop spawning and start to drop back out of the river there will be no bars to block them. They will ride the current down to the Thompson and from there back to the sea. They will not stop to feed or rest. "They'll go as fast as the current will take them," says Caverly.

By mid-July, in two short months, the fry will begin emerging from the gravel. As many as 50 percent of the eggs may not survive. The rate of production would be higher if the stream were in better shape. Floods will scour out some of the redds, grinding up the fragile, orange eggs. Sediment will be a major cause of mortality in the early stages of life. Soil washed from broken banks will physically block the emergence of fry from the gravel, and it will kill more by reducing the amount of dissolved oxygen in the intergravel water. By preventing interchange with surface water, blankets of sediment will literally suffocate eggs in their beds. The fry that do survive will probably emerge into a relatively clean and productive stream. By July, water levels will be down and the sediment load should have cleared, as long as there isn't further disturbance by road building, logging, or by ranchers driving equipment into the river to reclaim land.

But the fry will still face problems. The long sunny days that help clear the stream also start to wither crops on the flat bottom lands. As ranchers irrigate their fields, using diversion ditches and pumps that drive water into long aluminum sprinkler pipes, they will draw down the Deadman dramatically. The stream, already stripped of its shade trees, will start to heat up rapidly. Some small fish will get caught in landlocked pools where they will suffocate or be eaten by predators. Others will get killed by the heat. In recent years, irrigation ditches have fallen out of favour as a method of getting water onto fields. That has been a blessing, because the ditches unintentionally diverted hundreds of thousands of fish out of the main stream, then left them stranded in the mud when the ditches were drained onto the fields. There are still many ditches in use, although it is a crude and environmentally devastating process. Fisheries biologists plead with land owners to think of the fish, but have little authority to stop the practice. Under water lease rights, ranchers can draw down the whole river if they want to.

"The water here has all been licensed. The watershed has been licensed away. In the summer, in a drought year, they are capable of withdrawing all the water," says Ian McGregor. "In most years they might withdraw 50 percent. When that happens you get high water temperatures and that causes severe stress in fish."

≈

Water has always been a problem in this arid landscape. Marring the steep slopes above the river is the track of an old flume that once ran down to orchards on the sagebrush benches above the Thompson. Gentlemen farmers from England tried to start an Eden there, but the flume never functioned properly, with most of the water evaporating before it reached the fruit trees, and the dream of Walhachin turned to dust. The men went away to World War I and the flume fell apart.

Without liberal water rights some of the small ranches in the Deadman Chasm might also fail. But by running the tap unchecked, ranchers are threatening an incredibly valuable and rare resource. For 14 years, since the secret of the river was uncovered, the governments of B.C. and Canada have ignored the problem while steelhead numbers have dwindled. Before it is too late, politicians must weigh the relative values and then answer this question: what's more important, the production of a few more steers or the preservation of a unique run of wild steelhead?

The ranchers themselves don't face any moral dilemma. The river eats away at their land so they take a Cat into the stream and reroute the channel. Their alfalfa fields start to dry out, so

they pump the Deadman up onto the flat fields. Let the steelhead take care of themselves.

"The ranchers don't feel the same way about steelhead that I
do. They don't value them," says McGregor. He pulls his truck
over and looks out across the chasm towards the river. Right
there, he says, pointing his finger out the window, a day earlier,
he stopped a rancher who had driven his Cat into the stream to
push gravel from the river bed up against an eroding bank. Huge
clouds of silt poured downstream from around the grinding
treads and were churned up by the massive steel blade. The Cat
was in the river during the middle of the Deadman spawning
run, in the middle of some of the most important steelhead
spawning habitat in the world. A warning was issued, pictures
taken, charges contemplated. Upstream, that same week, another
rancher had built a dam right across the river to divert water
into his ditches. The dam was removed, charges contemplated.
Under the Fisheries Act it is illegal to deposit deleterious substances into fish habitat; it is also notoriously difficult to get
courts to take such matters seriously. After all, what's a few dead
fish? If convicted, the Cat driver might be fined $100.

I follow McGregor on foot across a field and along a fence
that has been strung by fisheries workers to keep cattle away
from the streambank. Vegetation is starting to spring up along
the water's edge. One day cottonwoods may grow here again, but
for now they are found only in log jams, where the discarded
trunks have washed together in deep piles. The bankside grass is
long, at least, and willows are taking root. We pass a series of
natural springs that bubble up in the fields and run through
thickets to the Deadman. The water entering from the springs is
cool and crystal clear. McGregor hopes the provincial government will buy the ranch on which these springs sit. For
$200,000 the government could get 3000 acres surrounding the
most valuable stretch of spawning gravel on the entire river. The

springs could be modified to provide perfect, stable spawning beds, a sanctuary — The Deadman Chasm Steelhead Sanctuary. McGregor, daydreaming for a moment, says he could see people coming here, just to watch the great fish. "You know," he says, "we could build a couple of artificial platforms so the fish would spawn right there in front of them. It could really be something."

He is moving quickly, surveying each pool with a glance. We pass the bleached skeleton of a steer. It seems prophetic. "This is a beautiful place to spawn," says McGregor, loping along a section where big cottonwoods overhang the stream on the far bank. "There should be fish all through here." There are not. "There's a redd," he says after a moment. Scooped out behind a granite boulder we can see an oval of clean gravel about half the size of a desk top. The collected silt has been swept away by the repeated arcing of a female's body. The male will have stood by, waiting for hours while she cleared the redd, attacking rival males, chasing away any trout that dared venture close. The redd is placed in knee-deep water where a swift run of current should keep it clean. As long as the silt load isn't too heavy, the eggs may hatch. We go farther up the stream, then turn, retrace our steps to the springs and start down on new water. We see one more redd, a rainbow trout hovering over it, either looking for loose eggs or planning to spawn in gravel cleared by the larger steelhead.

"This is a very fertile system. It has so much going for it," says McGregor, dismayed by the lack of spawning sign. "The Deadman produces the biggest fry in Canada, maybe in North America." The fry emerge in mid-July, small enough to rest on a fingernail. By September they'll be just over 3 inches — the length of an index finger and twice the size of fry from some other systems. Studies have found that larger fry have a 70 percent greater chance of surviving to adulthood than those that are even a few inches smaller.

The Deadman not only has the ability to produce bigger fry, but it also has the potential to produce more of them per redd than any other river. "The fish here are the most fecund in North America," says McGregor. Deadman steelhead have small eggs compared to steelhead elsewhere, but more of them. A doe in the Deadman will carry 12,000 eggs on average, while a fish of similar size in a coastal river will have only 3000. The fish on the Deadman evolved to take advantage of the natural state of the river. Coastal fish must carry fewer, larger eggs so that alevins can emerge attached to expansive yolk sacs. Coastal fish hatch in clear, sterile streams and need to carry more supplies with them for the first weeks of life. The steelhead of Deadman Chasm emerge into a river that is rich in aquatic life. As a stock, they should thrive. That they are not thriving is a condemnation of society's failure to recognize the importance of this special system, and to act to protect it. The biologists know what needs to be done, and so, clearly, do the steelhead.

McGregor stops at a house to say hello to the rancher whose property he hopes will become a sanctuary. "What are those fish called? Steelhead?" asks Pauline Docksteader, casting a skeptical eye at the river. She'd be happy to sell to the government, she says, long as the price is fair. McGregor says he'll get an appraiser in. "Oh, that don't matter to me," she says. "I know what it's worth." The ranch has been in the family since 1956. She mentions, just in passing, that when she was driving on the highway the other day she found herself behind a truck carrying bottled water. Would anyone, she wondered, be interested in bottling the water coming out of her springs? McGregor just shrugs. He knows one thing for sure. The steelhead could use that water a lot more.

Driving out of the chasm later, coming down over the sagebrush flats along the Thompson, McGregor recalls what it was like a decade ago, before the falldown began. One day, fly fishing on the big river, he caught and released 14 steelhead. It left his arms aching. Now experienced anglers fish five days, on average, to catch one fish. I told him about the big doe I caught at a run known as Martel, near Spences Bridge. "She was holding above the Nicola then," he says. "That means she was coming here, to the Deadman. She's probably in there right now." Of course I knew she was, and I knew where she spawned too — in the gravel runs near the fish fence, under the rainbow-coloured cliffs. That is, if the Cat didn't kill her.

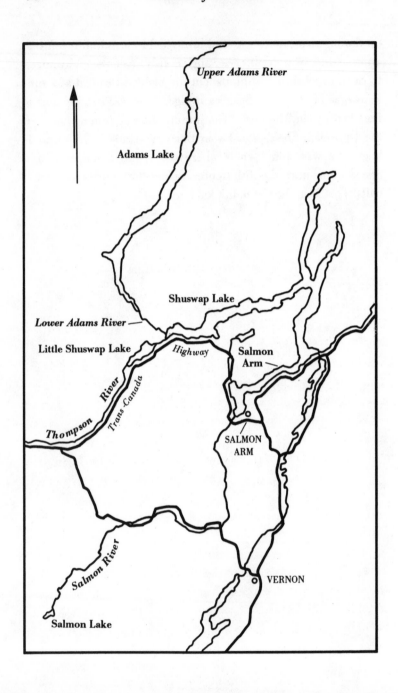

EXTINCTION AND THE GENETIC CODE

The Salmon and Adams

On a summer's night in 1905, one of the first fisheries officers in the Shuswap region of south-central British Columbia went searching for a great salmon run. David Salmond Mitchell went past the outlet of the famed Adams River, where the carcasses of spawned-out sockeye lay knee deep on the shore, and continued down Shuswap Lake until he reached a long inlet called Salmon Arm. At the head of the inlet, running out of a broad, picturesque valley, he found the mouth of a small stream that had been named, simply enough, Salmon. He rowed up the gentle, serpentine stream in the moonlight, his oars almost brushing the shore on each side of the boat. This is what he found:

"About a mile from its mouth I tied the bow to a long stake that was driven in the bed of the stream. There was no sign of salmon. I unrolled my blankets in the stern and went to sleep. Several times I awoke to listen and look around; there was no sound but the faint gurgle of the passing water around the bow.

"In the grey of early morning I was aroused by a commotion,

97

and found the river full of sockeye running upstream. I put in an oar and felt that the river was half fish. The increasing light soon showed that it was red from bank to bank.

"Then a stampede or panic occurred, and salmon came surging down, but the river was so full of ascending fish that they blockaded and made a great flat wriggling dam. So jammed were they that they crowded out, and were rushed up the sloping banks out of water. Where the banks steepened, these struggling flapping fish were rolled down onto the backs of the fish in the river bed below, into the mass of which they would again sink. The boat was on fish, on a red, flapping squirming mass.

"The fish lower down stream, suffocating for oxygen, had turned and were rushing back to the lake to breathe fresh water through their gills, and the mass subsided. They rushed down stream creating a great noise, like the roar of a storm, or the noise of thousands of wild ducks rising from a lake and followed down stream by a succession of waves. The river was quiet again, flowing by the stake 14 inches below the wet high water mark reached a few minutes before."

Eight years later that run of salmon was extinct.

Sockeye vanished from the Salmon River in 1913 after a series of rock slides blocked fish passage in the Fraser River at Hell's Gate. The slides, caused by railway construction, were disastrous to salmon stocks throughout the region, but particularly to the early running fish that came home during a time of low water, to the Salmon and the upper reaches of the Adams. Overfishing during the early 1900s also did immense damage. For several years, between 91 and 94 percent of the sockeye entering the Fraser were taken by commercial nets. And of course farmers took their share, pitch-forking them onto the fields along the Salmon River where crops still flourish today.

In 1952 — 39 years after the last red fish had been seen in the river — sockeye returned to the Salmon. There were 25 of them, barely enough to fill one small pool and a sad reminder of the seething mass that had lifted David Salmond Mitchell's boat that night on the river. But it was a remarkable sight nonetheless — because they were sockeye.

One of the immutable laws of nature is that extinction is forever. Despite appearances, however, there has been no miracle on the Salmon. The genetic strain of sockeye that was unique to the river, that was so perfectly adapted that it flooded the banks, is gone.

The red fish that came back in 1952 and that, off and on, have continued to reappear in the Salmon (none in 1989, a few hundred in 1990), are believed to be colonizing fish that have spilled over from big sockeye runs in the nearby Adams River. Salmon in the lower Adams fared better during the Fraser slides because they came back later in the year, in October, when the water was higher and passage was possible. The sockeye run in the Salmon now appears late in the fall, coinciding with the Adams, not during midsummer as it once did. But at least sockeye are back in the Salmon, which has given hope to the people of the valley. They want to see the river full of fish again, but first they will have to rebuild what was once one of the most productive spawning rivers in the province, for after the sockeye run vanished, the habitat was badly abused.

≈

The Salmon River rises in dry grasslands on the Douglas Plateau, where cattle wander across dusty roads and old ranch buildings are weathered the colour of copper. It drops through a rocky gully with scree slopes and brown clearcuts marring surrounding hills, before winding through a rich agricultural valley system to enter Shuswap Lake at the town of Salmon Arm.

The river is full with the promise of salmon, but wading downstream between green farm fields, I find the pools empty, the gravel beds covered with silt. Then I sight a glint of silver under a far bank. A salmon. I wade slowly across the shallows, expecting it to dart for cover. It doesn't move, and as I draw near I can see it has been wedged upright between some sticks. The salmon, a coho, is dead. I reach down into the warm water and pull the fish out by the tail. It is a perfectly formed salmon, silver and gray and unmarked. Slime runs off its nose and drips, glistening, into the river. The fish (one of 3000 coho and 1600 chinook that ran into the river this year) is carrying eggs, but it suffocated in the Salmon River before it had time to spawn.

The Salmon Arm district consists of gently rolling hills and fertile valleys set amidst the rugged Columbia Mountains. The flat bottom lands have been pressed into production by hobby and commercial farmers who raise cattle, dairy herds, field crops, and fruit and vegetables. There is a turf farm on the lower river, and a fallow deer ranch near the headwaters. There's a cheese factory and a small rabbit ranch. There are, in the fall, fields that stand tall with corn and fields littered with surplus melons and squash. There's a pick-your-own pumpkin patch that boasts 6000 pumpkins.

In all there are about 37,000 hectares of agricultural land, supporting some 800 farms. All of the farms need water, and if they don't get it from wells that tap the ground table, many of them draw it directly from the Salmon.

≈

Jack Stead parks his '81 Jeep near an abandoned bridge and leads me through a melon patch along the lower river, near where Salmond Mitchell moored his boat on that incredible, moonlit night. A retired school administrator and active target shooter, Stead is president of the Salmon Arm Fish and Game Club.

"This field was completely underwater during the spring," he said. "Water running everywhere."

Passing a small pumphouse with pipes drawing water from

the river, he notes that everyone seems to be taking a piece of the Salmon, even farms that disappear under floods early in the year.

Pushing through chest-high grass, he reaches the bank and peers down into the river. "That's it, you see. That's part of the problem. It's nothing but silt."

The riverbed is covered with fine sand and muck; there is nowhere for salmon to spawn. Without riverside vegetation to stabilize the shoreline, the river is eroding its banks, filling in the spawning beds. Fish need clean gravel to spawn in so that water can percolate oxygen down to the eggs. Without that, the eggs suffocate. And without adequate shade, the river heats up so much that the salmon fry that do hatch can suffocate in the summer months, just as mature salmon can die in the fall. The river sometimes gets so hot (over 21 degrees Celsius) that spawning salmon turn away at the mouth, repulsed by a current they instinctively know could be fatal.

"The problems on this river are numerous. It's not just water quality, which is affected by logging and agricultural run-off, it's also water quantity. The third thing is bank erosion due to spring flooding, and the fourth is the absence of vegetation along the stream," says Stead.

Upstream we find a small dairy farm where the Holsteins have trampled paths into the water.

"Now we see a feed lot and everything from it drains straight into the river. Every time it rains, that whole business leaches into the river," he gestures distastefully to the lot where cow pies and urine have been pulped into the mud. "That would make a helluva photograph."

We look upstream to where cattle are standing knee deep in the river, seemingly perplexed at our interest in them.

"Oh boy," says Stead, shaking his head.

The cattle eat streamside vegetation and further destabilize the banks by pounding pathways to the water. Run-off washes animal wastes and fertilizer from streamside fields, increasing the phosphate and bacterial levels in the Salmon River.

The solution to the cattle problem is to fence off the stream-banks, but that is cheap to talk about and expensive to do. Few farmers have surplus land, and fewer still have money to spare. A 1984 Ministry of Agriculture study of the area found that 50 percent of the farmers in the region needed off-farm jobs to supplement their incomes; 68 percent had yearly sales of less than $10,000.

It is clear that any solutions to the problems on the Salmon River will need the support of farmers who control the land surrounding the watercourse. And the solutions will have to be cost-free to the farmers.

"A lot of farmers don't give a damn. They are struggling too hard to make a living. But there are lots who do think about the river — we'll concentrate on the ones who care," says Stead.

His group is part of a remarkable project aimed at restoring the Salmon River as a major fish producing system. The Salmon River Project has drawn together a coalition that includes the federal, provincial and civic governments, the Salmon Arm Bay Nature Enhancement Society, the Shuswap Nation Tribal Council, the Neskainlith Indian band, Shuswap Advocates for Youth, and the Salmon Arm Fish and Game Club.

The Indian band started by raising 2000 seedlings of fast-growing dogwood and red osier to plant along riverbanks.

The district of Salmon Arm began discussing extending its main sewage line to the reserve at the river's mouth, which would, among other things, eliminate septic tank leakage into the river.

The provincial Ministry of the Environment promised water quality and groundwater drawdown studies, and was working to stop further water licences from being issued.

The federal department of fisheries had its biologists studying the river, and the Environment Youth Corps was surveying land owners "to collect suggestions/ideas on potential solutions to erosion, cattle access, pollution, etc."

The Fish and Game Club, which rebuilt trout spawning beds with great success at nearby White Lake, was ready to provide volunteer labour to put up fences or rebuild streambanks.

"We're going to pull together on this," says Stead. "It's going to work. We'll get this river back. Maybe not in my lifetime, but we'll get it back."

≅

Dave Moore, fisheries director of the Shuswap Nation Tribal Council, is sitting in his small office almost under the bell tower in the old residential school at Kamloops. From the front door he can look out on the Thompson River, up which passes one of the greatest salmon runs in the world — the Adams River sockeye run, which sees more than one million fish return in dominant years.

There are those who say the Salmon River's run of sockeye was once as plentiful.

"What went wrong with the Salmon River is what went wrong with fisheries management throughout British Columbia," says Moore. While stocks were being overharvested by commercial fishermen, habitat was being degraded. The salmon were being worn away at both ends of the life cycle.

"The Salmon River is a classic case of conflicting demands," said Moore. "The agricultural requirements had taken priority over the environmental requirements — and they eventually collided." Extinction was the result.

As part of the Shuswap Nation's overall strategy to revive traditional native commercial fisheries in the region, Moore looked at the Salmon River and wondered how his organization could help get the system restored. The tribal council had succeeded in

getting widespread community support for enhancement work
on the Deadman River, west of Kamloops, and now saw the opportunity for a similar project on the Salmon.

"Something we recognized in the Salmon River valley right
away was that there was a lot of community work on the river,
but it was frustratingly fragmented . . . Everybody was interested,
but they were doing their own little thing. The problem was,
each one had its own definition of the problem and its own definition of the solution. And none of them had the resources to
really tackle anything on a significant scale."

So the talking started. And from that, eventually, was born a
realization that all those who loved the river would have to work
together if they were going to get anywhere. Out of all the meetings the coalition was born in 1991, and the Salmon River
Project got underway. Perhaps the most hopeful thing about the
project is that it is not government-led. The people of the
Salmon Valley aren't sitting back waiting for the Department of
Fisheries to come in with a massive salvage operation — they're
doing the work themselves, with shovels and seedlings and the
cooperation of riverside land owners.

"If we were to go in with engineers and technicians, followed
by an endless line of dump trucks loaded with rip-rap, we
wouldn't get at the underlying problem, of the community looking after its own environment," said Moore. "Here we have
bands working with the various communities to create a con-
structive forum for residents experiencing the problems on the
Salmon River. It has really opened the doors of communications,
and that is vital because the agricultural community has its concerns, the native community has theirs, Ducks Unlimited theirs,
sports fishermen theirs . . . you have to look for a way to share a
common goal."

Moore said that, according to the elders, the Salmon River
used to support an early summer sockeye run, as did the Upper

Adams River. Sockeye running into the lower Adams are late fall fish, arriving in mid-October. The early-run fish were the target of native fisheries because they carried more fat and were better eating.

"The sockeye coming back in the Salmon River now shouldn't be mistaken for anything other than strays from other systems," says Moore. He wishes he was wrong about that, because if the Salmon River's original genetic strain was still intact it would make restoration of the river a lot easier.

"It's not beyond repair," said Moore. "We'll start at square one, with the habitat. If we can recreate the kind of conditions that the Salmon River had, the healthy, wild environment that was once there, then we can look at stocks."

Will the Salmon ever turn red with sockeye, the way it did in Salmond Mitchell's time? "Who knows?" says Moore. "But it's a worthy goal."

≈

The difficulty of reestablishing salmon in a river has clearly been demonstrated on the Upper Adams, where biologists have been struggling for nearly 50 years to restore a run that was once massive.

The lower Adams River is still known for its huge salmon runs. Every October, thousands of people flock to the viewing trails in the Roderick Haig-Brown Conservation Area to watch the sockeye spawn. It is a symphony of abundance in a beautifully pristine little river that the government wisely moved to protect, in 1977, because of concerns about land development.

Groves of huge black cottonwoods, trembling aspens, white birch, spruce, fir, pine and larch stand along the stable riverbanks. The clean gravel bottoms stir with the swirling bodies of sockeye that hold in such deep schools the water turns red.

Above the river stands Adams Lake, a long, cold body of water set between steep mountains. When the glaciers retreated up the valley, the ice in the lake was the last to melt. Salmon followed, eventually colonizing Upper Adams River and other tributaries. About 10,000 years passed before a logging company built a dam across the Upper Adams in 1907. The dam was used to store water which was suddenly released to flash-float logs down the river. Between flash floods, intermittent riverbed drying, and a steadily increasing commercial harvest downstream on the Fraser, the Upper Adams sockeye, like those in the Salmon, didn't have much of a chance.

As with the Salmon River, the slides at Hell's Gate created devastating passage problems from 1911 to 1915. Fraser River water levels were such that early-run sockeye were most seriously affected. Many of the late-running lower Adams fish managed to get through, which is why the Adams run is still of a significant size.

In a paper detailing attempts to reestablish Upper Adams sockeye, department of fisheries biologist Ian Williams notes a 1913 fisheries report that shows how suddenly the fish vanished.

"The run of sockeye to Adams Lake in August and September of 1901, 1905, and 1909 was so great that every tributary of the lake . . . was crowded with spawning salmon. I visited the headwaters in 1905 and 1909 and saw countless thousands of dead and spawning fish there. An inspection this year showed very few salmon on any of the beds."

Wrote Williams: "The splash dam on the Adams River ceased to operate in 1922 and was removed in 1945. Fishways were completed at Hell's Gate in 1946. While these corrective measures have been chiefly responsible for the success of the famous Adams River sockeye populations . . . field observations from 1941 and 1950-53 revealed no sockeye spawning in the Upper Adams system. Therefore, with no evidence that an indigenous sockeye population remained in the Upper Adams River, the International Pacific Salmon Fisheries Commission (IPSFC) began a series of transplants of eggs and young in an attempt to restore this valuable summer run."

With the habitat problems resolved, and sockeye thriving in the lower Adams, it might have seemed that restoring the upper river would be a simple matter. Such things in nature never are simple, as fisheries managers soon were reminded.

Two Fraser River tributary populations, Seymour and Taseko river stock, were used as donor species for transplants to the Upper Adams from 1949 to 1975. More than 10 million eggs and one million fingerlings were transplanted — but only a handful of them ever returned as adults.

There were moments of promise, but most years brought bleak results. In 1954, for example, 495,000 eggs were transplanted into the Upper Adams — but only 291 spawners returned, and many of them were wild strays from another system. Still, that was encouraging compared to what happened to the 1959 deposit of 1.5 million eggs: only five spawners came back. And there were many years with fewer fish than that. In 1975 more than two million eggs were planted in the gravel beds of the Upper Adams — not a single sockeye returned to spawn. The years of 1950, '51, '52, '53, '55, '57, '59, '61, '65, '67, '69, '71, '73, '77, '79, '81, and '83 were all blanks. Only in 1954, '58, '80, '82 and '84 did more than 100 sockeye return.

The Seymour and Taseko River stocks were selected because, like the Upper Adams run, they were fish that travelled great distances to get to the spawning beds. The Upper Adams is about 520 kilometres from the mouth of the Fraser River, while the Seymour sockeye run 540 kilometres to their redds; Taseko fish travel 664 kilometres. It became obvious after many years, however, that that similarity wasn't enough. The fish just weren't taking, despite massive egg transplants.

In 1980, biologists started experimenting with a third donor stock, Cayenne Creek sockeye, from a tributary of the Momich

River which enters Adams Lake near the Upper Adams. The Cayenne fish were from a similar habitat, ran a similar distance to spawn and had comparable timing to the Upper Adams runs — which is to say they came in early in the summer rather than late in the fall.

The timing of spawning runs is crucial to the survival of salmon fry because it determines when the young fry will emerge from the gravel and enter the lakes in which they spend the first year of life. The key to lake survival is the amount of nutrients available, and that differs from system to system. If the salmon fry arrive in a lake too early, they may die before food sources bloom in the spring. If they arrive too late, they can miss the peak of the zooplankton blooms and not build up enough strength to make their great migrations to the sea.

The crucial nature of timing was demonstrated for biologists at Karluk Lake, in Alaska, where an enormous sockeye salmon stock was wiped out by overfishing. The Karluk run went from 5.6 million fish in the 1880s to 500,000 over the last 35 years.

The potential of Karluk, like the potential of the Upper Adams, was so immense that biologists spent a lot of time trying to restore the stock. After decades of frustrating failure, fish scientists in Alaska began to think of Karluk as a Rubic's cube. They knew there had to be a solution; it was just a matter of getting the pattern aligned properly.

In a 1985 paper, J.P. Koenings and R.D. Burkett, of the Alaska department of fish and game, said they came to realize the key to the puzzle lay not in the river, but in the lake below and in the timing of fry emergence.

All prior attempts had focused on getting more adults back to the spawning grounds, but Koenings and Burkett noted this wasn't translating into an increase in the number of smolts exiting the system for the ocean.

What they came to understand was that the Karluk stock had

once been comprised of up to 20 separate groups of sockeye, all of which were intricately adapted to the environment. The groups spawned at different times, and the timing of their fry emergence was perfectly synchronized to the forage production in the lake.

In effect then, what the Karluk sockeye were doing was producing fry that converged on the lake in waves over the summer after emergence, making optimum use of the nutrients available. Overfishing reduced the Karluk stock to three or four age groups, and then enhancement efforts had concentrated on propagating those groups. The result, in simple terms, was that fry arrived in the lake in a few great lumps, causing overcompetition for nutrients at some times, and leaving the lake lightly used at others. The fish were out of synch with the lake — and the result was poor survival for fry.

≈

In the Upper Adams, biologists are faced with an even more complex problem. Instead of a relatively large run that has been reduced to two or three groups, they have been working to rebuild a system that was completely wiped out. All the sockeye stocks of the Upper Adams are extinct. The Fraser River slides and the logging flash-dam had destroyed not just a run of salmon, but a unique genetic program. The code to unlock the timing of Adams Lake had been erased from nature's memory bank.

In 1980, federal biologists turned to the nearby Momich-Cayenne system, hoping to find fish that were similar enough they could reestablish an Upper Adams genetic code. Two plants of fry totaling 727,000 were moved from Cayenne to Upper Adams. It would be four years before the results were known.

In 1981 there were 63 spawners in the once-great Upper Adams River. In 1982 there were 0. In 1983, 0 again. Then came 1984 and the adults from the Cayenne experiment came flood-

ing back through the lower Adams River, across Adams Lake
and into the Upper Adams — 3502 spawning sockeye — the biggest return since biologists had started working on the river 35
years earlier, and undoubtedly the biggest since extinction in
1913.

It will be years before biologists know if they have really repli-
cated the Upper Adams code. And they may never know for sure
if it was them or nature, because wild spawners have been trying
to recolonize the Upper Adams and it may have been their prog-
eny that sparked the rebound of '84.

An intriguing sidelight to this picture is found in the Momich-
Cayenne system in which, coincidentally, an early run of sockeye
reestablished itself while biologists were trying to get just such a
run to take in the Upper Adams. Did early-run fry that were released in Adams Lake simply home in on the Momich-Cayenne
instead of the Upper Adams? Prior to 1960 there were no early
fish recorded in Momich-Cayenne, but over the years a run did
get established, and it began to grow. Whatever the cause, the
Cayenne got a return of 5854 early sockeye in 1984, which was
just about enough to fill the creek to capacity and was nearly
double the previous high.

Ian Williams believes the key to the Upper Adams now lies in
continued transplants from the Momich-Cayenne, together with
a continuation of other efforts. Reviewing nearly 40 years of
work by the department of fisheries, Williams concludes: "If success is measured by commercially significant numbers of
returning adults, then these transplants were not effective. However, if success is measured by the creation of even a small
population, adapted to the Adams Lake watershed environment
and capable of providing seed for further expansion, then these
transplants were successful. The seemingly unsuccessful trans-
plant attempts in early years may have been important in
establishing a genetic base from which survival can be enhanced

using current biological and management technologies. A continued enhancement effort utilizing transplants, egg incubation technology, and improved short term rearing technology could result in a commercially viable run."

A run of just over 3000 salmon may not seem like much to show for nearly four decades work, but it is really a remarkable achievement given that the original genetic stock had taken an eon to develop.

There was a time when fisheries managers thought a sockeye was a sockeye; that a salmon from one river was not different from a salmon from another. Up until as late as the early 1970s, biologists were disputing the concept that there were many unique stocks within a species, although Willis Rich, of the Oregon fish commission, had argued for management based on stock as early as 1939. Scientists now widely accept that each stream has its own complex, individual environment, and fish stocks have evolved to match them.

For each system there is a special genetic code, and if biologists can crack it, fish may pour forth in a multitude. The Upper Adams could be reborn, and so too could the Salmon. The important thing is that the habitat is taken care of. Without that, no salmon can survive, for there is no genetic code that can overcome suffocation, pollution, or a lack of water.

In 1991 the American Fisheries Society did a survey of depleted Pacific salmon, steelhead and sea-run cutthroat trout stocks from California, Oregon, Idaho and Washington. The society compiled a list of 214 native, naturally spawning stocks — 101 of which were at high risk of extinction. Another 112 were listed as being at moderate risk or of special concern. Virtually the entire wild salmon population in the Pacific Northwest was in danger. No similar study has yet been done for British Columbia, but when it is it will probably show a disturbing trend in the same direction.

The society's conclusion about the cause of the problem, and about what needs to be done to fix it, is applicable anywhere in the industrialized world:

"The decline in native salmon, steelhead and sea-run cutthroat populations has resulted from habitat loss and damage, and inadequate passage and flows caused by hydropower, agriculture, logging, and other developments; overfishing, primarily of weaker stocks in mixed-stock fisheries and negative interactions with other fishes, including non-native hatchery salmon and steelhead. While some attempts at remedying these threats have been made, they have not been enough to prevent the broad decline of stocks across the West Coast. A new paradigm that advances habitat restoration and ecosystem function rather than hatchery production is needed for many of these stocks to survive and prosper into the next century."

It is not too late for the Salmon River. The stream that once ran red from bank to bank can be reborn. It will take a long and dedicated effort by the people of the Salmon Valley, but it can be done. And those that live along streams that still have wild stock might reflect on their importance — for once the code has been lost, finding it again is a monumental task.

THE GREAT
RIVER

The Stikine

Understand this about the Stikine: we are not just talking about a river here. We're talking about one of the most magnificent stretches of running water on the planet.

Born in the heart of British Columbia's wildest corner, it dies on the Alaska coast, braiding into channels that glisten like mercury on the tidal flats of Dry Strait. The Tlingit got it right, in the beginning, when they named it, simply, The Great River.

The Stikine rises on Spatsizi plateau, a Tahltan word for red goat. High on a mountain in what is now a wilderness park, white mountain goats roll in the dust of a huge sandstone formation, staining themselves a colour that has always been of ritualistic significance to Indians. Red ochre: symbol of blood, life, death.

The river starts in the alpine, runs north through pine forests, hooks back to the southwest and then pours through the Grand Canyon of the Stikine, where the great rock walls have been marked by engineers surveying for hydropower sites. As it makes its way to the coast it passes through towering mountains. In the lower reaches, just above where the Stikine crosses the border into the United States, a gushing white stream enters on the north bank. This tumbling, invigorating little river runs out of a meltwater lake at the base of Great Glacier, visible just above the willows that crowd the shore. The glacier, one of five in the area, falls almost into the Stikine itself.

The meltwater from Great Glacier runs over a bed of boulders scoured below the water line by the silt-laden current and softened above it by green moss hats. Long beards of moss hang from streambank trees. The glacier comes down like a dirty tongue out of the mountains, its crumbling face marked by deep blue cracks. Icebergs float slowly across the melt lake — some of them glistening and clear, others covered with gravel centuries old — and bit by bit they tumble down the small river to join the Stikine. You can sense a river being born here and feel the weight of time upon the earth.

Across the valley to the south, barely visible in the clouds, is a remnant of Choquette Glacier, named after the man who discovered gold on the river bars here in 1861. The two glaciers were once joined and the river ran underneath them. Salmon swam up under the ice and it is said that the Tahltans, when they came downriver, would send a woman alone in a canoe to see if the way was passable. Once the journey had begun there was no returning against the driving current of the Stikine. If she came out the other side the rest of the band followed, drifting their possessions down through a heart of blue ice. If she didn't reemerge, they would have to travel across the dangerous ice-field.

Some doubt the story, but to look on the river here is to believe that it's true. On the Stikine it's hard to separate myth and legend and history. Death is always close by. And it's impossible to take salmon out of any of it.

≅

As if trying to fathom the vastness of the terrain, regional

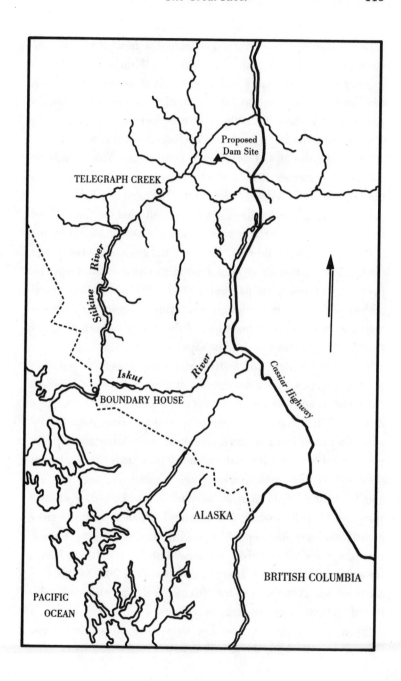

fisheries director Gordon Zealand runs his hand across a map covering the northern wall of his office in Whitehorse, Yukon. I was going in to the river with one of his fisheries officers that day, and had stopped to talk with him. Beneath his fingers passes northwestern B.C., the Yukon border and the Arctic Circle. He runs his hand from Prince Rupert on the central B.C. coast, all the way to the Beaufort Sea, where the Yukon ends on a desolate coastline. It is all his territory — a place literally and figuratively at the edge of the map. The northern fisheries region is a low priority for Canada, as reflected in the limited human and financial resources at Zealand's command. He covers the area with three officers, five seasonal guardians, two office staff, a habitat technician and a truck mechanic who keeps the fleet of battered pickups running. He has a $40,000 travel budget and goes bust on it each year without seeing all his territory. "In eight years stationed in Whitehorse I've seen lots, but there's still lots more to see," he says.

It's a big country. And to the federal department responsible for the region's rich salmon runs it is still largely unknown. "Some of these rivers, we don't even know what's in them," says Zealand with a shrug. Until recently, he might have added, Canada didn't care. For a century, salmon from transboundary rivers — so-called because they rise in Canada but cross the border on their way to the ocean — were taken without question by Alaskan fishermen. More than 50 percent of transboundary salmon spawn in Canadian water, but coming back to the coastal river mouths they are intercepted by walls of American nets. A small percentage are taken inriver, by Canadians. On the Yukon River, for example, Canadian fishermen take less than 20,000 chinook; Alaskans get 200,000. On the Stikine, with an estimated coho run of 50,000, Canadians take only 5000.

Even though international law states that salmon belong to the country of origin, the situation wasn't challenged by Canada until 1979. That year the federal government set out to promote commercial fishing in the Stikine and Taku, rivers so remote that fisheries officials in Vancouver describe them as being "a million miles from nowhere." For the next eight years, U.S. negotiators refused to budge on the issue, insisting that proprietary rights allowed them to catch all the salmon they wanted. They let through just enough to reproduce the runs. Canadian officials at first tried to negotiate higher catch quotas while managing the salmon to ensure the runs were not depleted. In other words, Canadians were only allowed to catch a small percentage because almost all of the fish that made it past American nets were needed on the spawning beds. The financial payback to Canada for taking this environmentally sound approach was almost nil, while the Americans profited. In 1987, growing frustrated, Canada announced it would increase its harvest levels regardless of the U.S. take — in effect, fishing down the number of salmon needed on the spawning beds. It meant possible destruction of the salmon runs. The gamble was made in the belief the U.S., which overall was taking 95 percent of transboundary salmon, would yield because it had far more to lose than Canada. It worked.

After expressing outrage, Americans agreed to a five-year deal, in 1988, regarding the Taku and Stikine. The Yukon remained in discussion; the Tatshenshini, where Americans take 200,000 salmon commercially while Canadians take none, had not been put on the table. Under the transboundary deal, Canadian and U.S. fishermen have their catch shares determined by a formula that fluctuates according to run strengths. If more fish are produced, Canadians will get a larger share. It is far from a satisfactory deal (Canada still only gets a small percentage of the fish it produces, not the 50 percent share that is due) but it is the first real sign the federal government cares about the great salmon rivers a million miles from nowhere. And if the Stikine is

ever enhanced to reach its potential, Canadian fishermen will be
the big winners.

≅

As the Cessna Turbo 206 lifted off a lake just outside Whitehorse, fisheries patrol officer John Burdek looked down at the
sparkling water of the Yukon River. "Chinook come up the fish-
way right here — 2300 miles from the ocean. It's kind of
incredible, isn't it?"

Burdek was on his way to the Stikine to check on a fisheries
officer who had spent the summer on the river, caught between
two warring camps of Canadian fishermen — one aligned with
the Great Glacier Salmon co-op, the other with the Tahltan fishing operation.

There are only two commercial groups on the river and both
set their nets just above the border, where the salmon are at
their freshest. Squeezing into a prime stretch of river only 10 or
20 kilometres long, the fishermen are in frequent conflict over
netting areas. The Stikine fishermen know that when they fight
they play into the hands of the Alaskans, for if the inriver fishery
dies, Canada will have no basis to argue for a bigger share of the
catch. A bigger allotment of fish would mean prosperity for the
Stikine fishermen, but that's in the future. On the river, the present is all that matters to fishermen fighting for economic
survival, competing for a share too small to let everyone prosper.

"It's a really strange atmosphere down there," said Burdek. "I
think it's the personalities involved and the fact you've got a lot
of money tied up in it. We were only 15 minutes into the August
sockeye fishery before we had our first fist fight right on the
beach. We do what we can. If it turns into an animal show down
there it affects them as much as us.

"It's just human nature. They work like dogs. They are mostly
good guys, but if you're going to go broke and starve . . . " He
leaves the sentence unfinished.

It takes a long time for Burdek to get from his office to the Stikine fisheries cabin, just upstream from the Alaska/B.C. border. About two hours into the flight he nods at the sea of white mountains and blue lakes that spreads to the horizon. "This is all my territory," he says. An hour later he nudges me. "Still my territory," he says.

As the Cessna comes in to the Stikine, Burdek warns Alkan Air pilot Pat Bruce that an aircraft sank on the river recently at the Great Glacier Salmon wharf. "It's wicked in there. The back eddy can tip you over and pull the wing right down until you go over." Bruce nods. When he lands on the burnished, gray waters of the Stikine he runs the plane's floats up against a beach far downstream.

It is late August, and at 10 p.m. darkness starts to slip into the valley of the Stikine, coming like a flood tide. Big cottonwoods skirt the river bank and spread across the narrow valley to the feet of the steep mountains — Choquette, The Knob, Sugarloaf, Katete and Iskut. On the water, Tahltan drift fishermen are still setting their nets just below Boundary House, a 60-year-old customs post built during the last gold rush that has now become a palace for mice and a temporary shelter for river people.

Ten minutes after they have dropped the nets over the side of their aluminum skiff, the fishermen race to catch up with the bright orange bobbers 500 metres downstream. On a heavy catch the floats sink as struggling salmon pull them beneath the surface. The coho are running now, thick-bodied fish as cold as ice, with a purple iridescence to them. Mixed in with the catch are some steelhead, lean and beautiful.

The fishermen live for the salmon, and they will be at work again before dawn, when a blue glow filters down the deep valleys to the east, softening the dark outlines of the mountains. Sitting on the front steps of Boundary House, I watch the light change for hours and can hardly believe the beauty.

≈

A few days later a boat pulls up to the old customs post. A fisherman with the Great Glacier Salmon co-op has come to fetch me.

Bob Gould, the driving force behind the co-op and one of its founding members, is waiting for me in his room at the Great Glacier plant just a few kilometres upstream. A solidly built man with a hard handshake, he tries to sound jovial, but there's an obvious sense of suspicion in his greeting. His fishermen had told him I was on the river. He wanted a few words. He wanted to get a few things straight, about Jonestown. About what the Tahltan fishermen had been saying, because he knew I'd been talking to them at the barge they lived on. About whatever it was Stephan Jacob, the head architect of the Tahltan operation, had said when he came to visit me at Boundary House. Yeah, he knew about the visit. He was a former military intelligence officer and nothing moved on the lower river without him knowing about it. First of all, about this Jonestown stuff. It wasn't true. He wasn't engaged in mind control. The 10 fishermen who were part of Great Glacier Salmon, which he'd founded, were equal members of the co-op. They thought for themselves. Sure they listened to him, because he'd started it all, with Jacob, when they were still friends and before Jacob went to work with the Indians, and because he'd invested so much of his own time and money. But the fishermen could think for themselves. Great Glacier isn't Jonestown, he said.

"Nobody's said anything about Jonestown," I replied. "Nobody's accused you of mind control. I've been talking to people about the transboundary dispute — about the sharing of the salmon resource."

Gould was expressionless. I saw his eyes measuring me. The military intelligence officer in him was looking for clues. He read whatever signs he could, then started to relax, started to talk about the river, about the fishing plant he'd carved out of the wilderness with the help of a small group of fishermen. They came in with pup tents and Coleman camp stoves in 1979, travelling in rented herring skiffs. They were following dreams of opening a whole new fishery and were inspired by federal government incentives. To get things going, the department of fisheries put up $100,000 in freight subsidies. That got the fishermen started. They didn't let go after that. After a second $100,000 in loans, the subsidies ran out for Great Glacier. Then the federal government, in an apparent attempt to right a previous wrong, gave $200,000 in subsidies to the Tahltans, who had been overlooked. Suddenly there were two competing fishing groups on a river that, because of U.S. interceptions, could only support one. Competition became fierce. Jacob went to work for the Tahltans. Hatred, anger and frustration followed. Some years were worse than others. This year was bad. Loaded guns in every boat. Fist fights. Near rammings. Through it all, Gould's obsession with the river and its potential never abated.

"Come on," he said. "I want to show you something. You carry the gun." He handed me a rifle with a piece of wire for a shoulder strap. We went out of his room at the back of the Great Glacier plant and headed into the bush. We were following a narrow path. It was getting dark. The path went almost straight up, beside a small pipe. "There's been a bear hanging around, but I haven't seen him in a few days," said Gould. I felt for the safety catch and found it with my thumb. Was it on or off? The wire cut into my shoulder. The gun barrel hit me on the back of the head when I jumped from a deadfall. At the top, sweating, we found a pool. The Great Glacier fishermen had dammed a stream and funneled it into a pipe. It fell down the hill and drove a generator that gave them hydropower.

"We carried the cement bags up on our backs. And the pipe. Once we had power we could do anything." Below us we could

see the roof of the sprawling Great Glacier plant with its dining
hall, aquaculture shed, processing facility and apartments for 10.
We could hear the hum of the power station that was driving the
lights, now blinking on, and the blast freezer, where salmon were
quick frozen and stacked like bricks. The backbreaking work
done by fishermen in establishing the Stikine operation has never
been fully appreciated by the federal government, says Gould. If
politicians could only stand here, above the wild river, and see
what a handful of people had done to wrestle a living from the
wilderness, politicians in Ottawa wouldn't be so complacent.

"Somebody has to start looking at this great space on the map
objectively," he said. "New Westminster [where DFO's Fraser
River and transboundary division is headquartered] has a conflict of interest in managing the Fraser River at the same time
they're managing the transboundary rivers. They focus everything on the mighty Fraser and they virtually have no interest in
this area. They are making budgetary decisions on the basis they
think the Fraser River is the greatest salmon-producing river in
the world. As far as the soap opera here, the blame has to fall on
DFO. They have created the conflict [between Great Glacier and
the Tahltans]. Meanwhile those guys down there," he jerked his
head west, towards Alaska, "are making glib use of Canadian waters and a Canadian resource and they think they own it."

I was struck at that moment by how much Gould sounded like
his old friend-become-enemy, Stephan Jacob. Visiting me at Boundary House earlier, bringing along three Tahltan body guards,
Jacob too had railed against DFO and the Alaskans. And he had
lamented the war between the two groups of inriver fishermen.

"The history of the Stikine is divide and collapse, divide and
fail. That's the history of this fishery. The fight between the
groups began in 1981. The war continued up to the point where
people were pointing at each other with guns . . . over fishing
holes; fighting over the resource; straight confrontation over

fish." Jacob, at one point, had been in a fist fight on the river. A Great Glacier fisherman jumped into his boat. They started punching. Jacob's head was held over the side, under the water. The heavy silt of the Stikine filtered through his hair, ran into his ears. "I've been afraid for my life," he says, his hands folded gently on the kitchen table. The Tahltans looked on silently.

The Stikine has immense potential, he said. If I could only see the tributary rivers, blocked by natural waterfalls. Blast them out and hundreds of kilometres of new spawning grounds would be opened. And then there are the huge beds of glacial gravel along the river. Divert water over that and massive spawning channels would be created. Just think of it. Seven million sockeye. Immense.

≈

Not everyone was drawn to the Stikine for profit. Marilyn and Doug Blanchard, of Francois Lake, first came up the river in the 1960s. They were looking for a place to spend their summers. A place that was wild and beautiful. They liked what they saw so much they built a tiny, one-room cabin on the banks of the river and have spent their summers there for more than 20 years. Dave Tauber, a young commercial fisherman with Great Glacier Salmon, wanted to run me up the river to visit the Blanchards.

"They are great people," said Tauber of the couple who probably have the only lawn on the river. "They always have a cup of coffee waiting."

We ran up in Tauber's salmon boat, passing beneath the Great Glacier and going past the mouth of the Iskut River. As we went he pointed out the drifts where he set his nets. "This is a great eddy right here," he said at one point. "There have been bad fights over this one." He didn't like the conflict on the river, but you had to stand up for your rights, he said, or you'd get pushed off the best water. He carried a 12-gauge pump shotgun behind his seat. The barrel was sawed short to make it easier to wield. The sun was out, the mountains shone and the glacier was blue. Tauber held his arms above his head and turned slowly around in the boat. "Isn't it beautiful?" he asked. "Isn't it the most incredible place you've ever seen?" He was not a violent man. The thing that bothered him most, he said, was that the Canadian government just didn't seem to give a God damn.

At the Blanchards', we tied the boat to some rocks on shore and walked along a narrow dirt path to the cabin. The couple greeted us on the doorstep as if they had been expecting visitors. Marilyn put the water on while Doug stoked his pipe and talked about life on the river. Geese woke them in the morning, coming in to browse on the grass, and moose stopped by in the evening. He pulled out a picture of a cow moose apparently engaged in pushing a lawn mower. He'd taken the shot from his door; the moose was licking salt from sweat left on the mower's handle. Behind the cabin, in a series of sheltered pools, schools of coho salmon fry flared and darted for cover as the shadow of a bird crossed the water. Just off the beach we could see Blanchard's fishnet bobbing in the silt-laden current. He was a set-netter rather than a drifter, and although he was a member of the Great Glacier co-op, tried his best to stay out of the emotional currents swirling around the commercial fishery.

He was worried about the war between fishing factions on the river and hoped it would be resolved by a permanent transboundary treaty that gave Canada a fair share. Beyond that he saw a more dangerous threat — the destruction of the river's salmon by mines.

"Everybody around here hopes they stay away," he said of resource developers who were trying to push a road down the Iskut Valley to the Stikine. Tauber agreed. They think the river's future is salmon. Tauber had walked most of the Stikine's tributaries. He had seen the water that could support the seven

million sockeye Gould and Jacob talked of. "The fishery potential of this river is staggering," said Blanchard. He and Tauber
said they hoped Canada and the U.S. could one day work together on the Stikine. But neither was optimistic. They had
heard too many years of talk. International cooperation so far
meant nothing more than agreeing to ship Canadian sockeye
eggs to Alaskan hatcheries to produce fry for restocking in the
Stikine and Taku systems. Still, you couldn't forget the potential.
Along its gravel bars and in its swirling back eddies the Stikine
constantly whispers of salmon — as once it did of placer gold.

≅

The headwaters of the Stikine are protected by Spatsizi Provincial Park, the tailout by the LeConte Wilderness Area,
established in Alaska in 1981. But in between, the river lies un-
guarded. Since 1979 a number of national and international
environmental groups have been fighting to preserve the full run
of the Stikine River. In 1985, Residents for a Free-Flowing
Stikine, Friends of the Stikine, Southeast Alaska Conservation
Committee, native people and government representatives met
at Telegraph Creek to discuss a proposal for a 3.5 million-hectare
Stikine National Park Reserve. The goal? Nothing less than a
park corridor along the entire river, including the Little Klappan
and Spatsizi tributaries. (The designation would stop mining and
logging, but allow commercial fishing.)

Hopes were high at first, but by 1986 Friends of the Stikine
was so alarmed the group published a newsletter declaring the
river was on the threshold of destruction. Because of a powerful
development lobby and a compliant provincial government, the
river has remained teetering on the edge.

Near where the mighty Iskut pours into the Stikine, a single
white cross stands on an outcrop of black rock. Erected in memory of a native fisherman who drowned, the cross serves as a
stark symbol of the river's possible future. In 1979, when the

Alaska Geographic Society published a book on the Stikine, it described the Iskut this way: "The great eastern arm — the domain of moose, wolves, goats and salmon — is seldom visited by humans today, although Tlingits and Tahltans once used the river extensively."

Today there are new tribes up the Iskut. The whack of helicopter rotors breaks the silence of the wilderness to announce the coming and going of mineral exploration parties. Some days it seems as if you are on a major chopper flyway. Up the Iskut, near Johnny Mountain, huge gold deposits are being delineated in an area now known as the Golden Triangle. The source of the placer gold that settled on the Stikine's bars has been found.

Skyline Explorations, a pioneering company in what was a full-scale gold rush by the late 1980s, started production with an underground operation tracing a series of mineral leads rich in gold, silver and copper. Staggering costs and start-up problems nearly closed the mine shortly after it opened in August 1988, but it reorganized in 1989 and was soon producing 350 tons of ore a day. In March 1990 alone it extracted 4531 ounces of gold, 8681 ounces of silver and 151,188 pounds of copper. Gold bars are poured on site, while the concentrate is flown out for shipment to a refinery in Japan. The mine has had trouble being profitable because of the remoteness of the location. From February to May 1989, the company spent $1.1 million transporting fuel and supplies to the mine. Despite such costs, and problems with the mine's overloaded cyanide leach circuit, the company has remained confident of success in the area. So have others.

One mining company described the Golden Triangle as "a 150 mile long belt of structurally controlled gold deposits... [with] proven reserves totalling over 6,000,000 ounces of contained gold."

Late in the fall of 1989 a significant gold discovery was made about 40 kilometres east of Johnny Mountain, at Eskay Creek, where Calpine Resources located one of the biggest finds in northwestern B.C. At the same time, Cominco Ltd. and Delaware Resources were developing the Snip deposit, believed to have 1.2 million tons of gold ore. North of Snip, Delaware, American Ore and Golden Band Resources were drilling. Granduc Mining was on the Sulphurets property, with two million tons of gold-bearing ore, and Gulf International had the McLymont property, with assays showing 0.810 ounces of gold to the ton. Soon more than 300 properties had been staked in the region.

Gold mines present a number of environmental concerns, not the least of which is the production of toxic cyanide. Mine engineers say the good news is that there are five proven techniques for removing free and complex cyanides from liquid mill effluent. The bad news is there are a lot more ways than that to spill it. The Iskut is a major salmon spawning stream and any effluent it carried would soon get into the Stikine. A toxic cyanide spill, or a mine leaching acid, could destroy both rivers and the dreams of people like Jacob, Gould, Tauber and the Blanchards.

What has kept most mines out of production so far is the remoteness of the region. The *Northern Miner*, a mining industry newspaper, describes the area as so rugged it "challenges the abilities of even the most experienced explorationists." That problem can be solved. In the spring of 1990 the Social Credit government of B.C. approved construction of a road down the Iskut. The road initially was to stop short of the Stikine, but with the valley of The Great River beckoning in the distance, it seemed unlikely it would really end there.

Peter Rowlands, Friends of the Stikine president, has been fighting to save The Great River for more than a decade. Developments up the Iskut scare him more than anything else.

"Our concern is that this road will never end, it will eventually find its way down the Iskut to the Stikine confluence and provide logging access."

Those who love the Stikine have seen what logging can do. Just south lies the Bell-Irving watershed along Highway 37, site of some of the most devastating clearcutting in the world. Entire valleys were stripped and the logs shipped whole to Japan.

Two small operations have already failed on the lower Stikine itself. Cottonwoods were clearcut to the water near the Iskut confluence as recently as the mid-eighties. Native groups, which are striving to establish economic foundations, are among those who want to log on the Stikine. So far they have agreed to restrict efforts to helicopter logging. It's unlikely that such logging will be profitable, however, given past experiences. The only way the Stikine can be logged economically is if the government heavily subsidizes roads into the area. That would mean turning the Iskut road into a mainline, with spurs into forest pockets along the Stikine. Roads visually destroy the wilderness, cause erosion, block fish from spawning streams and lead to overhunting and poaching.

There are more threats to The Great River. Upstream from the Iskut, above Telegraph Creek, lies the Grand Canyon. Pure white mountain goats can be seen on the black cliffs. The water through the canyon has been described as perhaps the wildest whitewater run in the world. B.C. Hydro has selected four possible dam sites: one in the canyon, one just below it, and two on the Iskut. Although the dams are not being actively pursued, Hydro is keeping a watchful eye on the rivers, monitoring flows for the day it wants to make more concrete plans. Officially the power company scoffs at suggestions it wants to build a dam in the near future, but as one Hydro executive puts it: "God made the Stikine to be dammed."

In 1988 there was a bright moment of hope for the Stikine when the provincial Ministry of Forests drafted its Lower Stikine River Recreational Corridor Management Plan. Environmentalists, native groups and other government agencies had contributed and all understood there would be no logging, mining, or road building from the Alaska Panhandle to Telegraph Creek.

Jim Munn, district manager for the Cassiar Forest District, and Jim Snetsinger, regional recreation officer for the B.C. Forest Service, have said that scenic and recreational values in the Stikine Valley are worth more than logging. (There are about 2000 hectares of harvestable spruce and cottonwood, worth approximately $300,000 in stumpage fees.)

"On a sunny day you can see the glaciers flowing right into the river. It's a beautiful place. It's well worth saving," said Munn.

Said Snetsinger: "To sum it all up for timber management, there would be no large-scale logging permitted in a recreational corridor along the lower Stikine ... We are willing to forgo any long-term logging interests in recognition of the scenic and recreational values."

But then the report went to the minister's office in Victoria. When the final draft was released, it held far different recommendations. Corridor Management Units were instead called Timber Management Units. Logging and mining were to be allowed, with road access, as long as development took place with a "Visual Quality Objective" in mind. The plan talked about "leave strips" along the Stikine. Such plans had been made along the Bell-Irving too, because Highway 37 is a tourist corridor to Alaska. But Visual Quality Objective logging there turned a beautiful drive into a nightmarish run through a lunar landscape.

Rosemary Fox of the Sierra Club was flabbergasted by the report. "The Ministry of Forests has subverted the public involvement process. It means it's wide open to development and without environmental protection," she said. "I was just shattered by it. I was taken aback and deeply disillusioned."

When asked to explain the report's changes, Snetsinger replied: "I'm not at liberty to talk about it."

It seemed obvious enough what had happened: the mining lobby had jammed its foot in the door before the Ministry of Forests and the Friends of the Stikine could protect The Great River.

Peter Rowlands realizes there's no way to stop mining in the region, but he still hopes to keep roads out of the Stikine Valley. And he hopes the only logging taking place will be by helicopter.

"There's room for other developments as long as it's done with the integrity of the watershed in mind — directly in and out of the water [by barge] not with roads. There's no reason we can't float ore down the river."

It was gold that first brought people up the Stikine, and now it's brought them back. During the rush of the 1800s, there was talk about a rail line down the valley to Alaska. Now they talk about a road. In time the new gold rush will die again. If the road isn't built, the wilderness will survive. And if the river itself is protected, the salmon will still be there.

There may be seven million sockeye running up the Stikine one day. Just imagine that. It all depends on whether Canada wants to dream about such things.

THE COLOUR
OF COPPER

The Tatshenshini

Each item of clothing is packed in a zip-lock freezer bag.
Socks. Long underwear. Shirts. Towel. I sit up late at night seal-
ing everything in plastic. After awhile it seems only sensible to
put my toothbrush in a zip-lock bag too. My backpack is lined
with heavy plastic, then the small bags are wrapped inside. When
I dream of the river it rustles like sheets of plastic in the wind.

"Expect to be wet nine days out of ten," advises my brother
Andrew, who ran the Tatshenshini with a Parks Canada crew
years earlier. "You cannot — just *can not* — stay dry on that
river."

"Get a wet suit," someone else advises.

"Double your life insurance."

"The Tat is cold. It's always cold. It's like the moon with
water running on it."

People react when they hear you are going to raft the Tatshenshini, although few have seen the river and most don't even know
where it is. Some just say, "Oh, man," and you're never sure if they

are expressing jealousy or writing you off as someone who won't be around much longer.

The Tatshenshini River runs through the most remote corner of British Columbia, cutting through an arrowhead of land that juts into the top end of the Alaska Panhandle. Near Skagway, the U.S. border pinches north towards the Yukon. A narrow neck of B.C. separates the two, then expands in what seems like a cartographic anomaly, creating a triangle of British Columbia inside Alaska.

This is a place of staggering geography, a fact recognized by the federal governments of Canada and the United States, by the Yukon territorial government and the state of Alaska, but ignored by British Columbia. To the north, the land of the Tatshenshini is protected by Canada's Kluane National Park. To the south, in Alaska, it is protected by Glacier Bay National Park and Preserve. But the heart of the Tatshenshini wilderness has no special status. In British Columbia the Tatshenshini corridor has been regarded as nothing more than underutilized real estate.

The Tat, as it is called by river rats, rises in northern B.C., curls into the Yukon, comes back to B.C., then joins with the mighty Alsek River before breaking through the Saint Elias Range of the Coast Mountains in Alaska. It is known by whitewater guides as one of the top three rivers in the world, up there with the Colorado, which runs through the Grand Canyon, and the Bio-Bio, which dissects the tropical jungles of Chile. American Rivers, a non-profit conservation society based in Washington, D.C., calls the Tatshenshini the wildest river in North America. The group also calls it the second most endangered river on the continent. Only the Colorado is of more concern, because the Grand Canyon is being damaged by the operations of a hydro dam.

Threatening the Tat is a proposed copper mine on a massive scale. Geddes Resources Ltd., of Toronto, made a pitch in 1990

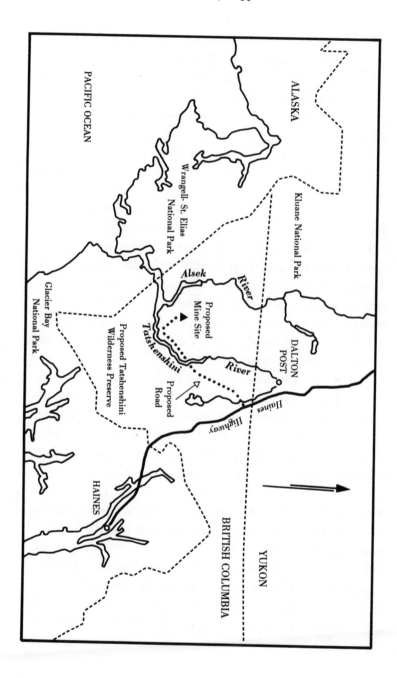

to open the area with a 100-kilometre road to a monstrous mineral deposit on Windy Craggy Mountain. If the price of copper holds, the Windy Craggy mine will last 20 years and create 600 jobs. A small city will be built in the middle of nowhere, roads and a slurry pipeline will pass through empty valleys, and Geddes will mine a copper deposit said to be worth five billion dollars.

The mine would be in the middle of a pristine wilderness that spreads over 930,000 hectares. An access road would parallel the river part way, then cross it with a bridge vaulting from bedrock to bedrock at a narrow spot now known as Monkeywrench Rapids. River runners have systematically ripped out survey flags there.

Under the Geddes plan, Windy Craggy Mountain would essentially be crushed and shipped to Japan. Waste rock would be dumped on nearby glaciers, or buried in a lake created by an impoundment dam. Mine supporters argue that, underwater, sealed off from oxygen, the sulphur-bearing rock will not generate acid drainage. They say it will be safe. But for how long? Ten years? Fifty? One hundred? What then?

The Tat has been untouched for 10,000 years, since the glaciers retreated, opening a corridor through the mountains to the sea. Now it is changing, prompting some profound questions. Should it be left wild? Can it be? What does Canada get if this great valley is opened for development? What will the world have lost when wilderness on this scale is gone?

≈

When we turn off the Whitehorse-Haines highway, it is raining. The windows in the van are fogged up and the 12 other rafters inside with me cannot see the river in the valley below. Three of them, guides with a commercial rafting company called Alaska Discovery, know it well enough. But the rest of us, a party of 10 zip-locked against the weather in rubberized rain suits, are straining to see out. On a steep grade the van stops. It is piled with gear, including three Havasu Professional whitewater rafts (deflated), and the driver is afraid it might run away, go straight past Dalton Post, and plunge into the Tatshenshini. She asks everyone to get out and walk.

Vancouver *Sun* photographer Nick Didlick and I are away first, unzipping layers of clothes as we run down the hill, going around a couple of bends and leaving the van behind. We see wolf tracks in the mud. Then bear sign. We hurry down across a clearing to a bridge over the Klukshu River. Below a fish-counting weir, a school of sockeye salmon gathers in the clear water. Some are in red spawning colours, but others are green and silver as if they have just left the sea, which is nearly 200 kilometres away on the Alaskan coast. On this day 1201 sockeye will pass through the fence. Local natives have an important salmon fishery on the Klukshu and just downstream, where the small river joins the Tatshenshini, non-native anglers gather in July for a chinook slaughter that tries to pass under the guise of sport. At the rafting put-in there are wooden gutting tables along the river, slanted so blood runs into the water. You can walk the bank and find empty Sportsman cigarette packages and crushed beer cans. We camp in the middle of this flotsam from the Tatshenshini zoo fishery, surrounded by signs that warn this is grizzly country.

The Tat has been a lost world for a long time. It did not develop into a travel route during the Klondike gold rush, unlike other big rivers like the Stikine to the south and the Yukon to the north. In 1898 about 300 people tried to reach the Klondike along the Tat, but only a dozen made it to Dalton Post, a trading station on the trail to Whitehorse. The rest turned back or died. Those that survived told a story of hardship, privation, sickness and death that kept others from following in their footsteps.

The first recorded trip down the river appears to have been made by Edward James Glave and Jack Dalton in the summer of 1890. Glave was exploring Alaska for *Frank Leslie's Illustrated Newspaper* and Dalton was a packer and guide, after whom Dal-

ton Post was named. Glave described wild rugged country that
has changed little since then.

"All this part of the country is suggestive of violence; these co-
lossal heaps of rock rudely hurled from the mountain heights,
the roaring and thundering of the internal forces of the glacier
and moraine, whole forests laid low by the fury of the tempests;
the wild, angry torrent of the Alsek River, roaring as it sweeps
past the desolate scenes — a combination framed by nature to
be inimical to life," wrote Glave in his colourful newspaper
account.

Although it is a major migration corridor for birds (including
Arctic terns passing through on 22,000-mile journeys) it has
been little used by people, even by natives. In the fall of 1991
the Champagne-Aishihik band sent a party down the river looking for sites some of the elders talked about. It had been so long
since anyone lived in the valley that nobody could remember exactly where to look for the old camps. But the salmon, like the
migratory birds, never stopped using the valley. It was their
home, as it was for the grizzly bears that roamed its sandbars and
denned in its cutbanks. Some say the river should be left for
them. What an incredible idea.

It wasn't until 1976 that commercial rafters first ran the river.
They were searching for new trip routes, but not much business
developed at first. The river was just too remote, too unknown.
Slowly word spread about the Tatshenshini, and then, in 1990,
Geddes made the river the focus of an international environmental debate when it proposed the mine. Since then, rafting
demand has greatly increased. Soon there were up to 36 commercial trips a year on the Tat, carrying from 200 to 400 people
in all. People were afraid the last wilderness was vanishing and
they wanted to see it before it was gone.

≈

The river is white with glacial silt. I cup a handful and drink it. It tastes almost sweet and I feel the granitic particles crunch between my teeth. The salmon, I'm thinking, have to swim blind in this, through canyons and rapids, past icebergs that tear at the river bottom as the current bulls them downstream, and over shallows haunted by bears. When they hit the clear water of the Klukshu it must be intoxicating. That night, I hear the real river in my dreams for the first time. It sounds like a big wind bending a forest low and it never stops.

On the morning of departure, lead guide Jeff Behan, with 80 runs through the Colorado's Grand Canyon and a handful of descents on the Tat behind him, calls the group together in a riverside grove of black cottonwoods. The rafts are tethered nearby, tugging like water buffalo at their leashes.

"What I am about to outline here is a worst case scenario," Behan says. "I don't expect any of this to happen." He talks about how to swim on your back, feet up, so you can watch where you are going. Don't fight the current; let it carry you diagonally to shore. Use your feet to deflect yourself from boulders. If you come to a log jam, roll over, swing your legs behind you, and thrust up so you aren't sucked underneath. If you try to fend off a log jam with your feet, the river will crush you. Hypothermia — in the cold waters of the Tat you have about one minute before coordination starts to go; in five you are so cold the body core is marginally functional. If you aren't out of the water in ten minutes, you might as well get sucked under a log jam because it won't make much difference. He talks about high siding; when a raft starts to flip you throw yourself across to prevent a capsizing. And he talks about bailing. "When I say bail I mean bail like hell. Get the water out . . . A swamped boat's a runaway freight train!"

Behan has a tough task. He has to reassure his clients and let them know they are going to have fun, but at the same time tell them that they could get killed.

"If this was a dangerous trip I wouldn't be doing it," he says, winding down. "I bill myself as a gentleman adventurer.

"The main thing about this whitewater rafting is — don't go out of the boat."

And he stresses that what we are going to see is worth the risk. "I heard a lot about the Tatshenshini when I was guide in the Grand Canyon. I had really high expectations when I first came here. But I didn't really expect it to be *that* good. It surpassed my highest hopes. Canadians should realize they have a Grand Canyon of their own, right here in British Columbia," he says, metaphorically. There are two canyons on the Tat, but neither is of staggering proportion. What the river has is a sweep of wilderness that leaves you with the same neck-aching dizziness and sense of insignificance that the Grand Canyon does.

While he talks, the river runs past behind him, relentless and fast. It races around a bend below camp into a canyon with rapids named Pinball and Twin Rocks, where rafts have high-sided and been broached; where kayaks have been cracked open like peanuts. One paddler lost his boat in the canyon and spent five days walking out.

In their guide *Rivers of the Yukon*, authors Ken Madsen and Graham Wilson praise the Tat for its incredible beauty but warn about "big weird water" that must be respected.

In the book *Rivergods*, Richard Bangs and Christian Kallen, among the first rafters to do the river, describe long stretches that are "a joy to run, a boatman's dream, a safe yet speedy shot between the ever-rising mountains." They also write about how, without warning, the river can offer "a fifty-yard stretch of monstrous boils, whirlpools, hydraulics, and souse holes, a virtual glossary of river dynamics . . . rendering the oars useless . . . We spun and lurched and filled with water."

In his 1890 story of the river, Glave tells of a native fisherman who counted off on his fingers the number of Indians drowned on the river. Glave later almost added to this list: "The water rushed in on all sides of us, threatening to swamp our little craft; it seemed for a moment or two that escape from the furious element was hopeless, but by powerful paddling we eventually emerged from the surging mass, all of us drenched through and through and the canoe filled with water despite energetic bailing."

Before we know it we are leaving Dalton Post, the ponderous rafts, loaded high with equipment, responding slowly to the slap of oars as we thread through a rock garden towards the canyon. Running around the raft is a rope to grab onto if you fall overboard. I wrap my left hand in it and find a second hold on the equipment pile in front of me. I am in Behan's raft, in the stern, with Jim (Stratto) Stratton, a representative of the Alaska Conservation Foundation. Our talk drops off as the river narrows and speeds between the rock walls.

The canyon is finished in a blur of time and whitewater. It is slightly less terrifying than the Dragon roller coaster in the kids' section at the Pacific National Exhibition. My left sock is wet, but otherwise I'm dry, while those in the bow have achieved their first "face plants," taking waves down their necks and sleeves. In a total face plant, the water runs all the way down inside your rubber rain suit, and fills your boots.

We drift down to camp, laughing, hearts beating, thinking there is nothing to be afraid of on this river. Guide Nels Niemi, a Tat veteran with 14 descents in 13 years, carefully builds a campfire on a fire pan so there will be no blackened rings of rocks when we leave in the morning. He will shake the ashes into the river. He collects all garbage and packs it in a box to be flown out later with the rafts. People are told to bury human waste after first burning the toilet paper, which otherwise decomposes slowly.

Guide Nancy Peel says that even that may not be good

enough. One day, she says, people floating the Tat will be asked to use plastic bags to collect their own waste so it can be packed out on "bag-it boats" as it is on the Colorado.

"I can see the day when we'll have shit boats on the Tat. We're certainly prepared to do that to protect what we've got here," she says. Geddes plans to leave all its shit behind: 18,000 tonnes of crushed waste rock a day, for 20 years.

Surrounding us are tumultuous ranges where most of the mountains have never been named, let alone climbed. Huge side valleys open along the river, and looking up them you see great forests that have never been logged. There are no roads. No seismic lines. No orange survey flags. There is so little human sign that when you see it, it's jarring. At one creek mouth, stopping for drinking water, I walk across a gravel bar, drawn by something that seems out of place back in the woods. In a small clearing there is a frame with a crossbar propped high off the ground. Nooses of rope hang down, stained a dark copper colour by old blood. Moose might have hung there, twisting slowly. Or wolves. The hunting campsite is dirty and there's a big fire ring and some rusting tin cans. I feel uneasy about what has been done here, and retreat to the rafts. We drift on, collecting firewood from sandbars as we go.

When we camp next it is on an outwash plain created by a creek that pours out of a deep canyon. On the distant granite cliffs we can see flecks of white. Mountain goats, just below the cloud line. Nick and I get our tent up quickly, grab his cameras and set off. There is a trail through the timber. It was once a narrow bear path (you can see old claw marks in the cottonwoods) but has now been widened by rafters who like the campsite below. We come out of the trees climbing straight up, going fast. After we make the first high point, Nick turns off to take scenic shots. The goats are still too high and far away. I go on, legs and lungs burning, then see a goat close. He tops a ridge, disappears, then comes out again 20 minutes later. Through binoculars I watch him climb without effort. He jumps a crevasse and stops to eat grass, looking gently back over one shoulder. Up here, with clouds drifting past and these great granite walls towering on all sides, it's clear the habitat is so extreme that no predators (except for human hunters) could ever pose a threat. God may not be a mountain goat, but you have to wonder sometimes.

Looking down I can see only one sign of humans, besides the tents and rafts far below; shining in the distance is the tin roof of a guide/outfitter's cabin. It is the only building on the Tat after the huts at Dalton Post. How can something so small, so insignificant, mar the view? I'm surprised at myself, but I feel the cabin has no place here. It is an intrusion in an unmarked valley. The next morning, as we pull out of camp, I look back to see if we have left any sign. There are boot tracks in the sand and I want to go back and sweep them away. A few good rains and they will be gone.

≈

In the spring of 1991 the Royal British Columbia Museum sent a survey party into the region for the first time. Wayne Campbell, chief ornithologist, came back raving about 27 species of mammals, 226 species of birds — and the landscape.

The research team found the Tatshenshini Valley to be the only place in B.C. where snow buntings, gray-cheeked thrushes, Arctic terns, northern shrike, and red-necked phalarope breed.

In his field notes Campbell scribbled: "Large populations of grizzly bears, moose, mountain goats, wolves, wolverine; only area in B.C. where all three species of ptarmigan (white tailed, rock and willow) can be seen on single mountain . . . Biologically little known area. Great discoveries yet to be made. Singing vole may occur — only place in Canada!"

On June 13, Campbell was on a six-hour hike alone, up near Big Shini Lake, when he ran into three wolves.

"They were also surprised," he later wrote, "and stood about 100 feet away curiously looking. Then they moved off north-wards and were joined by two more. These watched me from a clearing about 200 yards away, the three watched, only their heads showing, from among the willows above them. We watched each other for nearly 15 minutes when suddenly a cow moose with twin calves began walking towards me. I stood up, she saw me and raised her hackles — straight up. She slowly loped to-ward me, and I began to get worried. When about 100 yards away, and still moving toward me, I let a volley of BB shot go. She stopped, but didn't flinch. I howled — and she slowly am-bled back to her calves, and took them off in the direction of the wolves, which of course by now were long gone. Quite a drama!"

It was the sort of encounter that Campbell, John Cooper and Michael McNall came to expect. In their summary report, the trio from the museum's vertebrate zoology division would describe the Tatshenshini as a place, "where the natural world proceeds un-interrupted (wolves stalk moose, golden eagles prey on porcupines, grizzly bears lump their bodies over warm rocks/boulders.)"

≅

The wildlife comes up without warning. We drift around a bend and there's a grizzly, out on a wide expanse of gravel. The bear has its head down, swinging from side to side, its nose vacu-uming the air for a scent of us. It knows something is wrong and the golden-brown hairs on its shoulder hump bristle in the wind.

The grizzly is standing on the north shore of the Tat, just above its confluence with the Alsek. The air is filled with the roar of rivers and the bear cannot hear anything but moving water. We think his small eyes cannot see us on the south bank.

But he knows.

Then he charges. Into the river, feet churning. He is crossing from his side to ours and in that instant the comfortable line separating our world from his vanishes.

"Get the gun," shouts Behan, who has just nosed his raft ashore. But the gun is buried under equipment and there is no time to dig it out.

"I've got the bear spray," replies Nancy Peel, jumping out of her boat. She has a can of cayenne pepper in her hand. They run down the bank together. Ahead of them, Nick and Tom Knudson, a Sacramento *Bee* reporter, are crouched in the willows directly across from the bear. They were trying to get close for pictures when the bear made its sudden run.

Now they are frozen in the bush, the bear coming across fast, and it occurs to some of us that the grizzly is a three year old. Its mother, which can't be seen on the flats across the river, may be somewhere in the willows. On our side.

"Tom!" shouts Behan. "Tom! Come back!" Knudson is the closest to the bear, and perhaps the most inexperienced about such things. He can't hear above the sound of the river.

Nothing much happens after that. The current is more powerful than the grizzly which, whatever his intentions might have been, is swept far downstream before he comes ashore. Didlick and Knudson come back, grinning. Wow. That was fun.

Behan takes a deep breath. As lead guide, everything uncontrollable — weather, wildlife, whitewater — is his responsibility. If anyone gets killed it will be his fault. "I was worried," he admits, but in a few minutes the encounter is forgotten. There is something bigger than a grizzly coming at us. The Alsek. Roaring out of a broad, glaciated valley, it joins with the Tatshenshini to produce a river as wide as the Fraser, six times the volume of the Colorado.

It is turbid, troubled and filled with currents that can take you completely by surprise.

"Fast water today," says Peel, leaning into the oars. Her feet don't touch the floor, so she braces them against the gear piled in front of her. She uses the strength of her whole body to move the raft. "Faster. Bigger. It doesn't scare me. But I respect it. You never forget it is more powerful than you are."

Says Behan, standing up in his nearby raft, and looking into the distance: "This is not just great wilderness — it's some of the *last great wilderness* left in the world."

At one time there are 24 glaciers visible. Their tongues are dirty and cracked; there are pillars and spirals of snow; blue ice shines in the crevasses; when you get up on them you can hear the ice moan and crack and ring. The glaciers grind the mountains and wash them into the rivers. The Tat and the Alsek are so thick with flecks of granite that the water hisses as it runs underneath the raft. At times we hear the thump and rattle of boulders rolling down the river with us. Nancy says the river is singing.

There is no adequate way to describe the scenery. Surrounding the river are jagged mountains where glaciers are moving. At your feet, tufts of Arctic cotton, bear tracks and just there, a few feet from shore, the dark dorsal fins of a school of coho salmon, headed for Dalton Post.

The mountains are layered with colour. It is mid-September and fall is sweeping across the north. Along the valley floor are lush green cottonwoods, marbled with bright yellow willow thickets; above are great swatches of red fireweed and then bands of amber moss — finally the fresh snow, steepled and smooth.

Looking at this scene, where a $30 million road will cut across the mountain flanks if Geddes goes ahead, you have to wonder: How important is it that the world has another copper mine?

Stratto puts it another way. "Can't we just stop making pennies?" he asks.

≈

The Windy Craggy deposit is wider than a football field and runs through the heart of the mountain. It contains more than 85 million tons in upper Triassic pillow lava with a grading of 3 percent copper and 0.1 percent cobalt. There are lacings of gold and silver too. Geddes would take the top off Windy Craggy with an open pit operation, drop the ore through tunnels, then move it in a slurry line, mixed with water, to a plant 13 kilometres away. Copper concentrate would be shipped by truck (one huge B-train leaving every 20 minutes) or by slurry pipe to Haines. The mine would produce 30,000 tons of ore a day. The world, so awash in copper that it was worth only about $1 per pound in 1991, could rest easy, knowing that there would be no penny shortages for the foreseeable future.

But on the Tatshenshini, there would be problems. Sulphur-bearing rock will leach an acid concentrate when it is exposed to air and moisture. The process is known as acid rock drainage; once it starts it can last for centuries. To guard against that threat, Geddes proposes to fill the open pit with water after the copper is exhausted, and to create a huge impoundment behind a dam to bury acid-generating waste. The rocks in the lake would last forever, but would the dam? Certainly not. Once acid rock drainage starts at Windy Craggy — as surely it will — it could go on for a thousand years, pumping copper, zinc, arsenic and lead into the Tatshenshini, killing salmon fry where they collect in quiet backwaters. The acid drainage problem is not avoidable in perpetuity, but it could be controlled long enough that all the people responsible for it — the miners, politicians and investors — were gone before it started to poison the river. And that, of course, is exactly the plan.

At the mouth of the river, where 180 U.S. fishermen have commercial permits (intercepting fish bound for Canada, where no commercial harvest yet takes place), fisherman Paul Smith shared our campfire one night and fretted about his future.

"We're worried not if, but when we get a big spill, it's going to wipe out our salmon, wipe out our lifestyle," he said.

"I could go up there and get a mining job and make more

money than I do fishing," chipped in Ralph McSpadden, who has fished the Tat since 1981. "But it's not worth it. What would [a mine] do to this area? They are takin' my lifeline. I been fishin' for 15 to 20 years and I want to go on fishin'." He took a draw on a can of Bud and focused on something beyond the campfire. "It not only kills this place, it kills the whole Gulf of Alaska. A lot of people don't understand what is going to happen here."

Pat Pelleet, a Dry Bay fisherman since 1969, said Geddes must put up "millions and millions" for an environmental contingency fund if the mine goes ahead. And the company should be prepared to buy out the commercial licences if there are any problems. "There's some people here and you're not just going to drop a trillion gallons of waste water down on us and not recognize the people," he said angrily.

"There's no question whatever goes in the Tatshenshini/Alsek goes down the river and affects the fish," said Greg Dudgeon, a ranger with Glacier Bay National Park and Preserve, whose lands surround the lower river.

He said a community of about 300 springs up at the mouth of the river every year, when the set-netters, their families, fish buyers and plant operators move in. "It becomes one of the biggest communities on the Alaska coast for awhile," he says, with most people living in tents on the beach. About 4.5 million kilograms of salmon are processed each year at a small plant.

To rafters, the mine road is the main concern. It would vibrate under the wheels of 45-tonne haulage trucks, with three passing any given point each hour. You would hear them shifting gears throughout the valley. Try to contemplate the wilderness while that's going on. The road would also visually destroy the untouched image of the Tatshenshini, and divide wildlife ranges, forcing bears, sheep and moose to crisscross a four-lane dirt highway.

Jack Goodwin, a B.C. guide/outfitter who has the only cabin

on the Tat between Dalton Post and Dry Bay, sits drinking a cup of black coffee (the last milk long used up) and looking out at a vast, untouched valley. Beyond the picture window he can see the Alsek Range, where he went hiking a few days ago — 50 kilometres out and back.

"Legs still hurt," he says matter of factly.

He has a wary relationship with rafters running the Tat. They don't like his cabin much, and they don't want his clients killing game that rafting clients pay to see on the hoof. He doesn't like wilderness adventurers overrunning the country and trying to shoulder out hunters.

But they have a lot in common when it comes to Windy Craggy.

"I'm dead against it," says Goodwin, who built his cabin on the banks of the Tat with the help of three friends in the summer of 1991.

Tats Creek, down which the road would run to the river, is a prime denning spot for bears. Goodwin knows because he has walked it. The road would separate sheep from winter and summer ranges.

"I have to ask myself: What does British Columbia get out of this? Nothing but a big hole in the ground and abandoned 20 years from now, while we still have a road running all over the country." Goodwin looks outside. "You know, you go up those valleys — nobody's been up there. Is it worth losing our wilderness?"

≈

Standing in a camp at the base of Walker Glacier, Nels Niemi is getting warmed to the subject at hand. Niemi, with a bandanna tied around his long, silver hair, looks like Willie Nelson. He carries a sketch book with him on his floats, drawing out the lay of the rapids to remind himself, from season to season, how to get through with minimum effort and danger.

"As soon as there's a road at Tats Creek, someone will put a trail right down the river. I don't think we can have responsible use of the wilderness if that road is in," says Niemi, adjusting firelogs with the toe of his gumboot.

More people should see the Tatshenshini, he said, because it is too profound to be enjoyed by only an elite. But the road would destroy what makes the Tat special.

"You can't have roads and wilderness too. It's a contradiction in terms," says Eric Myers, an assistant to a state representative in the Alaska assembly, and a guest on the river trip.

"At the same time, we are elitist," says Niemi.

"Without a road, a finite number of people will experience it, but just having it here, knowing it exists, is an important thing too," replies Myers. "It's a reflection of our consumer society that people want to be able to drive to the wilderness the way you drive to the grocery store . . . It's totally consumerism. That's bullshit."

Stratto moves a firelog with his boot, then turns his back to the cloud of smoke that billows up. "In this area, because it is so remote, you are going to have to carve the heart out of a wilderness to put in that mine," he says, looking across the valley. "The mine does not belong here. You have to draw a line in the sand and say 'No'."

Robert Peel is sitting nearby on a rock, listening quietly. He turns his head away when asked his opinion, not wanting to get into it at first. He is enjoying the wilderness adventure as much as anyone on the trip, but he doesn't agree with a lot of what he's hearing. Good-naturedly, he gets up to join the fireside discussion. Roads help people get into wild country like this, he says. And besides, what's 20 years when you think in terms of centuries? After the mine is gone it will be hard to know it was even there.

"Over half the people in Haines are clamoring for this project. They see the roads getting wider, straighter. They see the jobs . . . then you have the old boys, who have been around since time began. There were mines everywhere in their day. It's an argument that the wilderness can recover. You are right, it shouldn't be screwed up in the first place. But . . . "

Peel, a retired teacher and father-in-law of guide Nancy Peel, reminds us of a popular bumper sticker that pretty much sums up the attitudes of a lot of Alaskans: "Oh, Lord, give us just one more boom and we promise not to piss it away this time."

"For so long the mining and petroleum industry has operated under the belief that if it's out there, we have a God-given right to go and get it. Things have changed," protests Stratto.

"Here's the question," replies Peel. "How much wilderness is enough?"

"There's never enough," says Stratto. "We've got a finite amount of country left. We're going to fight for every bit of it because we'll never win it all . . . in 200 or 300 years maybe all this can be reassessed."

Peel holds up his arms, a gesture to the vastness of wilderness that surrounds the campsite: "You don't think there's enough? Seems like there's a lot to me."

Stratto nods acknowledgement of the point. As far as you can see in every direction there is nothing but wilderness. "In Alaska there's a lot left. But on a global scale, I mean, you go down to Oregon, where I'm from, and they are fighting over 5 to 10 percent of what is left. So industry has used 90 percent and they are fighting to get the rest? Give me a break. So much of what we had is gone. The pie is almost eaten up."

The next day, after we break camp and load all our gear inside zip-lock baggies, inside waterproof packs, inside rubber stuff sacks called "Bill's Bags," I ask Nancy Peel where she stands on the mine issue. She hadn't entered into the debate around the campfire, but she'd obviously been thinking about it and didn't hesitate to answer.

"I'm against it, but I don't have any factual reasons. It's

purely emotional. Anytime you open up an area it's just going to get trashed . . . you'll have mom and pop mining operations, you'll get ski-do trails, you'll get every yahoo in a 4X4, you'll get woodcutting. It loses something. I don't think every area should be accessible to every person. In the long, long run, we are dependent on the quality of our water . . . ultimately we are just shitting in our own back yard. They say, 'Oh, it's just one more watershed, one more watershed.' People only look at how it's going to fill or empty their pockets — and we need more vision than that."

Without a road, the only way to travel through the Tatshenshini Valley is the river. It is not easy. It starts with the canyon run just below Dalton Post and then, waiting for you 10 days later at the end of the trip, is a place guides call the Channel of Death. The day before we reach the channel, a plane flies low overhead. It's piloted by an Alaska Discovery guide taking advantage of a rare clear day to fly the river. Niemi gets the plane on a handheld radio, then shouts out to the other rafts, "Pete said: 'Don't go. There is no way. There be no channel!' "

The Channel of Death, which leads into a huge bend called Alsek Lake, is choked with ice. The glaciers crumbling into the lake have had a surge, filling the Tatshenshini with icebergs. The river runs under the ice.

"Go into the lake, you don't come back," says Niemi.

Under the leadership of Behan, the party of three rafts, with 13 people aboard, crosses the river at the head of the channel and goes down a narrow, shallow run to the north. It seems to be leading us nowhere and soon the rafts are grounded in ankle-deep water. A portage, involving a ton of equipment, looms ahead. It is Friday the thirteenth. The thirteenth hour. We stop for lunch. Niemi walks across the mud flats and looks out at the icebergs.

"Even a burned-out old veteran like myself, after 13 years

guiding on the Tat, has to say 'Oh, yeah. Wow! Look at that be-hemoth!" We stand and listen to the glacier calving into the lake and I'm pondering the recurrence of the number 13.

Nothing much happens after that. No bad luck, despite the numbers. We drag the rafts a short way, then the water deepens and we find we have detoured around the wall of ice. The Chan-nel of Death, like the charging grizzly, was a false threat. But drifting down to the final takeout at Dry Bay, with huge icebergs washing down with us, I am still feeling uneasy, thinking about Windy Craggy and wondering what the future will hold.

The prevailing political mood in British Columbia is to try and have a bit of everything. The government will want to have the copper mine and the wilderness too. But that is impossible. It must be one or the other. The mine will bring short-term pros-perity to a few; a national park boundary around the Tatshenshini would create the biggest international wilderness preserve on the planet — forever. In 500 years, people could still drift the river and see what I saw, the natural world uninterrupted. What an in-credible idea.

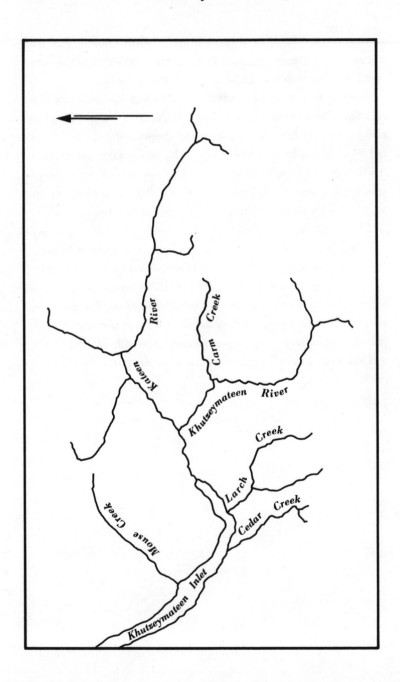

VALLEY OF THE GRIZZLIES

The Khutzeymateen

When Wayne McCrory built a platform for watching bears
in the valley of the grizzlies, he put it in the middle of a skunk
cabbage patch. Next to the spindly framework of steel piping ran
a spawning channel where sockeye salmon writhed in the shallows. He knew the bears had been browsing on the skunk
cabbage because it looked like an army of itinerant workers had
been through, turning over the rich, black earth with shovels
digging for potatoes. Each scoop marked the single swipe of a
paw. The gravel bars were littered with dead salmon, most with
single, delicate wounds where bears had nibbled out their nut-
sized brains.

During the salmon run, grizzlies all along the Pacific Coast
forget their aggressive territoriality and gather on streams to
feast. There are few places in the world where bears collect in
such numbers as they do in the Khutzeymateen Valley, on British Columbia's central coast.

McCrory, one of Canada's leading grizzly biologists, had long
heard about the valley of bears, 45 kilometres northeast of

Prince Rupert in the Western Kitimat Ranges of the Coast Mountains. But when he first went there, in the mid-1980s, he wasn't prepared for what he was about to discover.

"There was bear sign everywhere," he recalled. "There were bears in the estuary, bears in the forest, bears along the river. It is an incredible place for grizzlies."

Over the course of three years, McCrory spent 100 days observing bears in the valley. He concluded that the Khutzeymateen was such a unique place it should become Canada's first grizzly sanctuary. The idea had a lot of opposition, because the narrow valley bottoms that were of prime importance to the bears also held old-growth Sitka spruce, a climax rainforest 800 years old that was wanted by coastal sawmills.

On the night before my first day on the viewing platform, I sat with McCrory and two other bear biologists, Dick Russell and Erica Mallam, in the candlelit cabin of a small yacht in the estuary and talked about bears. Outside it was raining and dark; I wondered what the grizzlies were doing.

Russell, a senior biologist with the Canadian Wildlife Service, had come to the valley to assess the area for the federal government. He was interested in McCrory's approach to studying bears.

Getting up close to bears is always a problem for biologists, who have become increasingly drug and technology dependent. Knocking bears down with high-powered drugs and wiring them with radio collar transmitters has become the preferred method for many since it was pioneered by the Craighead brothers in Montana.

McCrory's method is much less intrusive. He basically moves in with the bears, either sitting on the viewing platform and waiting for them to come to him, or walking quietly through the woods along the river.

Russell thought McCrory's bear platform was a good idea, but he wasn't so foolish as to think it was perfectly safe. How long would the steel platform stand up to an assault from a bear?

"About two seconds," said Russell. He took a sip of scotch and grinned. McCrory would take me to the platform before dawn.

≈

We turned out of the fast water on the mainstem of the Khutzeymateen and paddled into a quiet back channel. Skunk cabbage leaves floated in the current. McCrory looked at them, looked at me, and held a finger to his lips. We left the inflatable, stumbled through the potholes in the cabbage patch and climbed up the platform in darkness.

At first there was only one sound and one colour. The pigment of giant Sitka spruce, hemlock, willow, wild crabapple, skunk cabbage, moss and sedges blurred together like green stones on the bottom of a river. The world was drenched with the colour of vegetation. The single sound, drowning out all else, was the frantic drumming of rain on the plywood roof.

McCrory had one leg tucked under him, like someone in a canoe. Mallam sat crosslegged, serene and contemplative, as if in a trance. Zen in the valley of grizzlies.

A few days earlier at the same place, McCrory, Mallam and Russell had watched a sow bear and two cubs rubbing against a tree. The rubbing tree was directly across the narrow channel and slightly beneath the platform. For the three veteran bear watchers it was an amazing sight — the sort of encounter McCrory has now come to expect in the valley.

Mallam had just got settled on the platform, with the others coming up behind her, when a dark brown bear came into sight 90 metres upstream.

"While she was still in the stream she was testing the air with her nose," Mallam recalled. "She went up the bank for about 10 minutes, we thought we'd scared her, but they came back on the trail, mother trailing two cubs, and started to use the rubbing tree."

The female stood on her hind legs, back to the trunk, scratching in obvious delight.

"I've never talked to anybody, or read anything from anybody, who's observed that before," said McCrory, a lanky, bearded man with the slow manner of a folk singer.

The tree, from years, perhaps decades of use, was rubbed smooth of bark, in places torn by claws to the heartwood. We later collected grizzly bear hair, trapped in globules of pitch on the trunk. Leading to and from the tree, and to other marked trees throughout the valley, were a series of gigantic footprints, twice the size of prints that would be left by the largest grizzly bear. McCrory said the prints were made by bears stepping deliberately in one another's paw marks. Bear biologists do not know why grizzlies do this; they do not know how many generations use the same tree and they do not know what it means to the bears when the rubbing trees are cut down. Biologists do not anthropomorphize, they do not attribute human meaning to the apparently ritualistic behaviour of grizzlies. But looking at that tree, rubbed smooth by great bears that had approached in single file, it was disturbing to recall what a hunter had once told me: when a bear is skinned out and hung up, it looks just like a human cadaver.

As light filtered into the narrow valley, the forest colours began to appear. Subtle shades of green and yellow, layered and mixed, emerged from the mist and the darkness. Once the rain stopped, the sound of water beating on the dense forest canopy was replaced by the distant roar of waterfalls. Far away, white ribbons appeared against black, glistening rock. It was up on those cliffs in 1920 that George Haimas, a native from Kincolith of Gitsees and Nishga ancestry, fell to his death while hunting mountain goats. That's how a sheer dark wall northeast of the river got its name: Where George Slid Down. A silver stream ran off the low end of the roof and poured into the skunk patch below us. A deluge, rushing from everywhere high to everywhere low, was turning the waters of the Khutzeymateen a muddy brown. When the tide changed, a line of dark water and flecks of white froth advanced down the inlet.

Mallam never took her eyes off the dense bush on the far side of the stream. A twig cracked, a sharp sound out of place in the dripping forest.

"Bear," she said.

McCrory cupped his ears and listened. The bear never came out of the woods, but you could hear it moving past. "This place is alive with sounds. So many different sounds," McCrory said in a whisper. The stream gurgled beneath the platform; salmon sloshed through the shallows. A sooty-gray American dipper gave a trill and dove into a pool, running along the bottom to hunt for salmon eggs. Overhead a flight of geese called as they went up the valley, bound for the small lakes at the head of Carm Creek. Merging with it all was the sound of water passing over stones, running through the great forest cover, dripping from the bent stalks of marsh grass, sedges and horsetail. The bears don't care about the rain. They wade in the river for the salmon and slouch through the drenched meadows. If they are hungry, they come out to feed. There have been as many as eight grizzlies spotted in the estuary at one time. Black bears are common as well. The first day we sat on the platform for 12 hours and never saw a bear.

≈

The Khutzeymateen was first proposed as a possible grizzly bear reserve back in the early 1970s, but it wasn't until about 15 years later, when logging interests began to press for access, that a handful of biologists, including McCrory and Mallam, began seriously studying the narrow valley.

Khutzeymateen (koots-ma-teen) is an anglicization of a Tsimshian term. Those who wish to protect the valley have translated it to mean "a confined space of salmon and bears." But the Gitsees, who trace generations of use back through the valley, have a less romantic reading. They say it's based on the Tsimshian words k'its'm adiin and means "in valley," which is the feeling you get when you turn into the inlet that leads to the river.

The Gitsees are a Coast Tsimshian tribe that traces its claim back to an unknown day when a great warrior named Haimas obtained the Khutzeymateen from the Tlingit. The legend says the valley was paid to him in ransom. Beyond that, the Khutzeymateen really belongs to Knagudze, a chief of the great monsters of the Sea World, who was told to move there by the other chiefs. He was to make Khutzeymateen his home and was told not to harm anyone and to lead a peaceful life. The Gitsees, or "People of the Seal Trap," have long used the valley for fishing, hunting, trapping, gardening and gathering wild plant foods. They built smokehouses near the mouth of the river and used them until about 1940, when the site was abandoned. The potato patches have been taken over by skunk cabbage, and the crabapples and raspberries have gone wild. The grizzlies continue the harvest.

The north Pacific Coast, including Alaska, with its high precipitation, dense rainforests, salmon rivers and rich marine environments, has the most productive grizzly bear systems in the world. While grizzlies in the interior have home ranges of about 900 square kilometres, coastal grizzlies roam habitat so rich they need only about 400 square kilometres.

The Khutzeymateen, with its huge salmon runs and flourishing sedge flats, is believed to concentrate bears from a vast mountain kingdom, funnelling them into the narrow valley to feed on fish in the fall and to browse wild grasses, the buds of devil's club, lady fern fiddleheads and other plants in spring. Most observations of bears are made on the estuary or along the lower reaches of the river where the terrain is more open. Indian trappers, however, say the biggest concentration of bears was always upriver, along the Kateen, a northern tributary. The Indians called the Kateen the "home town" of the grizzly. A radio-tracking program undertaken by B.C. government biologists located bears along the full length of the Khutzeymateen and its tributaries, with the soundings clustered along the narrow valley bottoms, precisely where the main timber harvest would focus. The radio-tracking program found some bears had relatively small home ranges, but others, like a 14-year-old male named B.J., covered 217 square kilometres and probably ranged much farther. The tracking program, which relied on the live trapping and drugging of bears so collars could be put on, provided hard data on 15 animals. It is through the program that we know the size of Grizzly Male 11's hind foot: 28 centimetres long by 17.5 centimetres wide (about 12 inches by 7 inches). And we know that Grizzly Male 32 weighed 300 kilograms (660 pounds) and had a neck girth of 99 centimetres (39 inches). Unclear is how many bears visit the valley seasonally and how many live and den there. But one thing became certain in the early stages of research: the Khutzeymateen has a lot of grizzlies.

"There are other places where you can find grizzlies on the coast, but this is the last of the best of the unlogged," McCrory told me as we sat together on his bear platform one morning, waiting for the forest to move. Bears crept by on either side, screened by the bush, their heavy feet snapping twigs.

"It is a special place for bears. Logging in this confined valley will destroy Canada's last chance to have a representative coastal grizzly bear sanctuary of international significance," says McCrory.

Once, while I waited alone, a shaggy brown head emerged from undergrowth, peering through the rain at the platform. The black eyes shone and seemed to look directly at me. As silently as it came, the head cautiously withdrew. If it was GM11, his skull was 44.4 centimetres long and the distance between the zygomatic bones on either cheek was 27 centimetres. Standing on his hind legs, GM11's broad face would have reached halfway to my perch.

I was shivering from the cold when McCrory came back at dusk and had no important sightings to report. He nodded when I told him about the head. "I think we'll rest the platform for a few days and explore the river. We may have disturbed this site too much. They'll come back into the open after we've rested it some."

≅

The tide comes in, the mud flats disappear. Delicate white gulls with gray backs circle above. A herd of seals that has been resting at the river mouth, surrounded by a cloud of steam, humps beneath the surface and slides upstream in pursuit of salmon. Sloshing across the flats, Mallam leads us through the marsh grass to a small mudhole. It is warm to the touch. A grizzly hot tub. "It looks like a bison wallow from the prairies," says Russell, who grew up in the Rocky Mountain foothills of Alberta.

From the hot tub, a mud-stained trail leads through the grass to a point where a bear has denned under a giant, moss-draped Sitka spruce. The yellow beards of moss are bright against the sombre green of the tree. A total of 45 well-formed beds have been counted around the estuary. "They sure pick nice places to camp," says McCrory as he stands under the shelter of the branches. His voice is not without envy. McCrory's tent, drooping in the downpour, is across the inlet on a steep pitch of land where small rivulets of run-off carve a web of channels in the earth.

Mallam leads the group on to Larch Creek, a frothy, ephemeral stream plunging down from a precipitous black rock mountain with slopes of 40 to 100 percent, along which a road must be blasted if logging is to take place. In the middle of the hunt for the biggest carnivore in the west, Mallam stops to point out a winter wren's nest; in a hanging ball of moss is a small entrance hole just big enough for two fingers. The nest is dry and warm on the inside. The wren, a tiny, secretive bird that fills the woods with a rapid series of melodious trills, has flown.

≈

The Khutzeymateen falls and rises with the tide near the mouth, and it falls and rises with the rains above that. It winds around gravel bars where wolf tracks have showered down in layers. Salmon carcasses litter the shore and catch like white ribbons in the log jams. At one bend in the river, two huge broken snags stand like pillars. Atop each jagged trunk, hundreds of feet in the air, a pair of eagles look down. Drifting into the quiet water behind, we find a deep hole where the current drops dead salmon on a gravel bar. The eagles fall like vultures to feed.

With our inflatable boat struggling against the current, we round a bend to see a huge black seal roll off a log in the middle of the river. About us, draped in the current, are the giant leaves of devil's club, each the size of a seat cushion. Amazonia in the temperate zone.

Travelling alone with McCrory through this wilderness, stopping to follow bear trails into the underbrush, I realize I have left more than the modern world behind — back there, somewhere in my other life, also lies the fear I once had of bears. Coastal grizzlies can weigh 400 kilograms or more. They typically charge on four legs and can run at least 50 kilometres an hour. They are good climbers and often stand on their hind legs, enabling them to reach as high as your average bear viewing platform. As any camper can tell you, they like to come around at night and breathe heavily outside your tent. Despite this, we are sneaking about as if coastal grizzlies are as vulnerable as winter wrens.

In a way they are. Black bears have proven adaptable to the

disruptions caused by humans, but grizzlies appear far more susceptible. Whenever resource development takes place in grizzly habitat, the road access leads to increased contact with humans and that means increased hunting, poaching and problem encounters — all of which usually add up to dead grizzlies.

Two researchers, Andrew Trites and Harvey Thommasen, who did a survey of grizzly deaths on the central coast, reported that 392 bears were killed between 1975 and 1988. Of that number, 55 were shot by non-hunters, either illegally or due to animal control. Disturbingly, there was not only a steady increase in the numbers of bears killed, but also indications that many bear deaths simply weren't being recorded. In the Bella Coola watershed alone, 89 grizzlies were killed but only 32 were officially registered. The researchers said most of the grizzlies were killed by local people who considered them to be problem bears.

Access to the Khutzeymateen is now difficult and expensive, but if logging goes ahead, a network of roads will be blasted down the steep slopes of the inlet and laced up the flanks of the valley where the biggest trees are found. Bruce Sieffert, a planning and inventory director for the B.C. Forest Service, has estimated the Khutzeymateen has 3.2 million cubic feet of marketable timber, worth between $7 million and $12 million in stumpage fees to the Crown. Because of the rugged terrain, however, professional foresters have disagreed over whether the valley can actually be logged at a profit. Consultant Herb Hammond has estimated losses of $6.3 million before stumpage fees, raising the possibility of a logging operation that would create work but would generate no direct revenue for the government. This has not dulled industry's appetite for the Khutzeymateen.

Foreseeing the dangers of logging, scientists as early as 1972 were trying to save the valley, unsuccessfully proposing it as an ecological reserve under the International Biological Program. In the late 1980s, with public pressure building to save the valley, the Social Credit government of the day agreed to let provincial carnivore biologists undertake a three-year study before making any final decisions. The government made it clear, however, that the only acceptable plan would be one that protected both bears and the jobs of loggers.

McCrory says the two are incompatible. "In every recent case where new forestry development occurred in coastal grizzly habitat, an apparent decline in grizzly populations has also occurred," he says. His opinion on what will happen if logging takes place is unequivocal: "Should logging roads be built in the Khutzeymateen, it will be very difficult to control poaching. Considering this, and the extent of other predicted logging impacts, grizzly populations in the Khutzeymateen would undergo a decline."

Nobody knows exactly how many grizzly bears use the Khutzeymateen, but it is estimated there may be 50. There are thought to be 6500 grizzlies in B.C., but the great bears are now extinct from the southwestern range of the province to California, terrain they once roamed freely. In North America the grizzly has been eliminated from over one-half of its natural habitat, and in the U.S. the population has dropped from 100,000 to 800 in the lower 48 states.

≈

Far upstream, with the green depths of the river below us and the forest towering above, McCrory and I beach his inflatable on a gravel bar. We watch salmon in the river, then wander through a promising thicket until McCrory stops. The yellow plastic bag he usually has over his model 870 Remington 12-gauge shotgun is pulled gently off. "I smell bear," he says. Drifting through the underbrush is a distinctive, musky smell that is unlike anything I've ever smelled before. "Those first few whiffs just stop you dead in your tracks. There's no mistaking it," says McCrory in a quiet voice. We press on but soon stop un-

der a Sitka, much like the one on the estuary under which a
bear had camped. Rain thunders on the forest canopy, but here
it is dry, like the inside of the wren's nest. McCrory digs his
hands into the earth. "A bear's den. Let's make ourselves at
home, but keep your ears open," he says with a slightly nutty
grin.

We eat our lunch and listen to the forest. The longer you listen, the more you hear. Over the years, McCrory says, he's
developed a sixth sense about bears. "I sometimes get a feeling
that I shouldn't be here. I get chills down my spine and the hair
on the back of my neck stands on end."

He ignored that feeling once, when he was doing hazard
evaluation work for the B.C. parks branch. He sensed a bear was
near but couldn't see it. Suddenly a grizzly came out of the willows in front of him.

"I looked at the bear and he was huge. I thought: 'You just
keep going and I won't shoot.' I hadn't completely got that
thought out when he jumped me. I got one shot off . . . and fell
backwards 15 feet down a bank." McCrory lay on the ground,
half dazed, the gun somewhere in the brush, waiting for the bear
to come charging over the top. After what seemed like a long
time waiting for his life to end, he slowly got up, found the gun,
then climbed the bank.

"He was there, lying behind a log. I'd heard grizzlies would
sometimes do that, and then jump you when you came in. I shot
him again . . . he let out a big roar, rolled over and died. It made
me feel awful to kill him. I just hated it. It made me evaluate
what I was doing and question if I wasn't pushing too hard."
McCrory stopped talking and looked out at the forest. The last
slow rattle of rain that follows a downpour was falling through
the trees. We were near where provincial biologists had returned
to a bear trap to find a dead three-year-old male grizzly. Held by
one paw in a snare, he had been attacked by another bear during

the night; there were bite marks and puncture wounds on the skull, neck and sides; the body cavity had been split open and the viscera partially consumed.

"I keep hearing other noises. It makes me feel nervous," said McCrory. He got up, whooped and went to check a thick patch of salmon berries; the branches had been pulled over and broken, the leaves and fruit stripped off.

≈

Late on the afternoon of the last day we heard the plane long before we saw it. Finally it came down out of the clouds that hid the peaks of the mountains, a single-engine Beaver dropping slowly into the green valley and landing at the river mouth. McCrory stood on the shore, the plastic bag over his shotgun, and waved goodbye.

The pilot, who had just failed in an attempt to fly in to nearby Ryan Lake to pick up goat hunters, leaned over and cinched my belt tight with a sharp jerk just before we took off. "It's going to be rough. It'll be like riding a bronco," he said.

The plane bucked, slid sideways on its tail, stood on one wing, dropped suddenly and bounced back up — all this before we reached the end of Khutzeymateen Inlet. We were in valley the whole way, with mountains close on either side. We came out of the inlet to Steamer Passage like a wild horse coming out of a wooden chute. The Beaver banged through the weather, out around the point and south down Chatham Sound to Prince Rupert. We followed the twisting coast rather than cutting up over the mountains of Tsimpsean Peninsula. "Too much cloud," said the pilot. "This way's twice as long, but it's safer."

It was rough all the way. High winds, sheared off by the mountains, had created a backwash of turbulence. Just outside Rupert we saw our first logging road, brown and muddy, twisting through big open patches of land. There was no forest canopy to slow the rain. Clearcuts were moving north. There were booms along the coast after that, simple geometric patterns of cedar and spruce in the green water. Here and there a huge log stood out. I was thinking of those big trees up the Khutzeymateen, but couldn't for the life of me remember what a grizzly bear smelled like.

THE RIVER GUARDIANS

The Cowichan

Beneath Joe Saysell's boots, a thin layer of high-impact fibreglass curves up, bow and stern, into the characteristic arc of a drift boat. Beneath the boat a riverbed passes in a slow blur of gravel, rock, shadow and light. It is what is between the bottom of the boat and the bottom of the river that concerns him.

The Cowichan River, flowing precisely at its 40-year mean average of 45 cubic metres per second, is dropping rapidly and with it, the boat's hull is falling towards the rocks. In this drift of the river or a subsequent one, the boat will grind to a halt on a gravel bar and Joe, caught between gravity and a hard place, will have to get out and push. It will mark the end of his season as a fly fishing guide on one of British Columbia's best rivers, and it will come in the spring, early May, when trout fishing is at its prime. It bothers him that the end of his season has nothing to do with the availability of trout and everything to do with the availability of water. And it bothers him that the rhythm of the river is determined not by nature, but by the forest industry and something water managers call "the rule curve," which dewaters the river according to a formula. Unlike rivers draining the B.C. Interior, which flood in the spring, Vancouver Island's Cowichan reaches high water in winter. January rain, not spring snow-melt, is what drives the river to its peak. But in May the river should still be running high, not dropping to a point where drift boats can no longer navigate.

Looking at the verdant green hills of the Cowichan Valley, cloaked with second-growth Douglas fir, hemlock and lodgepole pine, it is hard to imagine a water shortage. Along the pastoral valley floor, which looks like lush English countryside, are dairy farms and hay fields surrounded by 50-year-old second-growth forest. Along the riverbank are pockets of old growth, huge cottonwoods draped with bearded lichen, and dense thickets of salal, red huckleberry, Oregon grape and twayblade. The vegetation flourishes in a mediterranean subhumid climate, and so does the river with its clear, slightly alkaline, oxygen-rich waters supporting ten species of salmon, trout and char. Above the river at an elevation of 159 metres is a large lake, also named Cowichan, that collects run-off from a vast mountain basin where 2000 millimetres of rain falls a year. Together with its main tributaries, Somenos and Quamichan creeks, Cowichan River drains an area of about 90,000 hectares or 350 square miles.

The flow of the Cowichan River is controlled by a weir, a low-level dam, built by B.C. Forest Products in 1956 and later taken over by Fletcher Challenge Canada Ltd., a New Zealand forest products company. The weir, which you can see just above the highway bridge in the village of Lake Cowichan, was built at the lake's outlet so the flow of the river could be stabilized over the course of a year.

Like other rivers on the Island, the Cowichan historically had extreme seasonal highs and lows, building to high water under winter rains, gradually tapering off through the spring when snow-melt supplemented the flow, then dropping over the long,

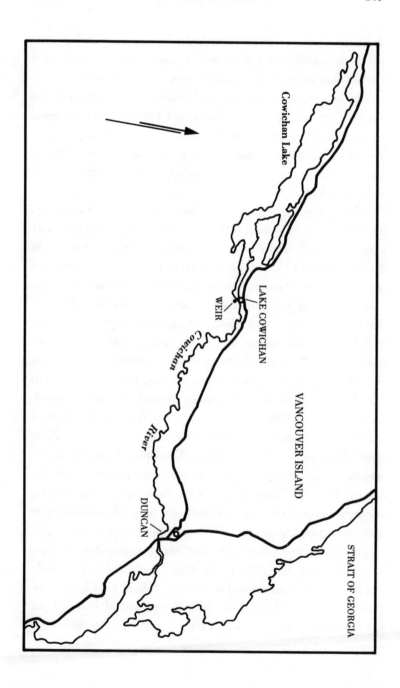

dry summers to reach low water in September and October. Late fall rains would bring the river up again. This natural cycle worked well for chinook, coho and steelhead, giving them freshets of high water in November and December when they entered the river to spawn. And it served the big trout that dropped down out of Cowichan Lake in the fall to feed on salmon eggs. The trout would stay through the spring, moving back to the lake only when the water level receded, which was often not until late June.

The natural cycle worked well for guides like Joe Saysell too, who remembers that before 1956 the trout fishing was good into early summer. In those days you could drift the river throughout May, a cushion of water carrying the boat over the shallows, following hatches of insects that brought brown trout, rainbows and cutthroat rising to the surface to take dry flies like the Grey Wulf, a bright, bristling imitation that floats high on the surface.

The seesawing nature of the Cowichan, however, was not good for a huge pulp mill that grew up on the shore of Georgia Strait on Vancouver Island's eastern shore, north of Duncan at Crofton. The mill needed a steady, dependable flow of water. Lots of it: 210 million litres a day. Once the weir was built, a 121-centimetre intake pipe was sunk into the Cowichan River about 8 kilometres above tidewater. The pipeline snaked 22 kilometres across the rolling countryside, disappeared into the labyrinth of the Crofton mill, then reemerged, after passing through a treatment plant, to discharge pulp fibre and dioxins into Osborn Bay, at the foot of a blue heron rookery.

Dave Heywood, industrial relations manager for Fletcher Challenge, said the Crofton mill simply could not operate without the pipeline and assured water flow. "There have been a few [dry] years where the mill would have run out of water [if the weir wasn't in place]," he said. "It's a fairly major part of our operation."

Water is used to dilute chips, debark trees and convey pulp fibre around the sprawling mill. It is sent through a million-dollar treatment plant before being discharged. The pulp mill is trying to cut down on the amount of water it requires to operate, but it is always going to need a lot because of the nature of the process. And the mill operators make no apology for that — as far as they are concerned, they aren't so much taking water from the Cowichan as they are borrowing it. "The water is heading to the sea — we just divert it," says Heywood.

The weir, which is equipped with gates and a boat lock, allowed the forest industry to raise the level of Cowichan Lake by about one metre, storing the water it needed in the summer over a surface area 41 kilometres long by 2 kilometres wide.

Once the weir was built, the flow of the Cowichan didn't change remarkably, but Water Survey of Canada streamflow records show a reduced run of water in the spring and slightly increased flows in the late summer to early fall. The roller-coaster flattened out, as the rule curve dictated a steady release of water after the full supply level was reached in the lake during April and May. Among the beneficial impacts was an increase in the minimum flow during the summer months, which helped fish survive the low, warm water of July and August.

≈

Biologists have found that coho production in the Cowichan is governed to a great extent by streamflow conditions during the time when juvenile salmon are resident in the river. As water levels drop and temperatures rise, the small fish become increasingly stressed and begin to fight over the dwindling habitat base. Many don't survive the summer. The Department of Fisheries once made a comparison between streamflow data and gillnet catch statistics from Juan de Fuca Strait, which is where Cowichan coho go after they have left the river and grown to size in the estuary. What they found were two graph lines that ran parallel across the charts. When water levels dropped sharply in the Cowichan, catch rates fell at an equal rate two years later, when the mature survivors were being harvested. When water levels were high, so was the commercial coho catch.

Under an agreement between the government and the Crofton mill, a fisheries "maintenance flow" of 7 cubic metres per second (cm/s) was established for May to September, increasing to 10 cm/s in mid-September to assist runs of spawning salmon.

The flow rates were calculated to ensure the survival of salmon during the summers, with increased flows in the fall to assist spawners. The levels, however, depended entirely on the amount of water stored in the lake, which, after some long, hot summers, wasn't much. In short, the agreement called for salmon to get extra water — *if the mill had it to spare.*

"Any management for fish is only if the weather cooperates. The first thing we have to do is see that the minimum flow for the mill is met," said Brian Tutty, a habitat biologist with the Department of Fisheries who has been working to improve conditions for spawning salmon.

Although biologists had long known of the important correlation between flow rates and fish survival, it wasn't until the late 1980s that they did something about the situation. A series of five dry years highlighted a serious chinook problem, making it clear that something had to be done to provide more water in the fall when chinook arrived to spawn. Water levels were so low for a few years that hundreds of big fish had been stranded in the estuary and lower river. Over the years the spawning run had fallen from 7500 chinook to 5000, then to 1200. By 1988 there was a real fear that the run could become extinct.

To ensure there was enough water in reserve, fisheries officials in 1988-89 had the regional water manager bend the rule curve slightly, to hold more water back in the spring when snowmelt and rainfall were spilling out of the lake.

That year, fisheries biologists tried an experiment on the Cowichan which gave them some promising results. After retaining the maximum amount of water possible over the summer, they had Fletcher Challenge open the weir in the fall, releasing stored water in a "pulse," hoping to trigger chinook that were holding in the estuary, waiting for rain.

Tutty was standing in the river the night the pulse came down. It was October 11, and the river rose around him, tripling its volume of flow from 7 cm/s to 21 cm/s. A fall freshet had just been created. To the salmon in Cowichan Bay it seemed like the real thing.

"It was dramatic . . . We literally had thousands of chinook coming up in ideal conditions," recalled Tutty. "It was essentially a manmade rainstorm. It triggered the fish. You could stand there on a gravel bar in the river and hear them come around the bend, 30- and 40-pound fish sloshing past."

A big salmon sounds like a bear when it comes upstream, splashing water onto dry gravel bars as it surges through the shallows. It was, to Tutty, the sound of a salmon run being reborn.

Saving spring run-off to release in the fall when it is needed most seems like a simple solution. Nature, however, is a lot more complex than that.

While fisheries biologists were trying to save the Cowichan's important salmon runs, provincial Ministry of the Environment biologists like Craig Wightman were working to protect the river's trout and steelhead. The Cowichan is remarkable in that, in addition to salmon, it supports three trout species, two species of char, and two runs of steelhead — one that arrives in November, another that comes in March.

George Reid, a B.C. government biologist and recreational fisheries manager, describes the Cowichan as "probably the most important river in British Columbia with that combination of brown trout, cutthroat and rainbows. It's rather unique in our region, and I think in B.C."

By swimming the river in snorkelling surveys, Wightman and other biologists determined that an absolute minimum flow of 7 cm/s was needed for trout and steelhead smolts during the summer months. To ensure that water was available, he agreed it was necessary to hold back water in the spring, even if it had a negative impact on the trout fishery. When the spring flow was reduced to 10 to 14 cm/s, big trout started to abandon the river, returning to the lake. Wightman said biologists would never knowingly jeopardize the survival of steelhead, but it was known that, once the river was below 14 cm/s, steelhead redds on shallow bars emerged from the water. If there were any eggs or recently hatched alevins in those nests, they would be killed. And dropping water also created landlocked pools in which salmon and trout fry became trapped. Small fish, surprisingly, don't know enough to swim to deeper water when a river drops around them.

Looking for a compromise, provincial biologists concluded that a flow of 14 to 16 cm/s from May 1 to June 15 would maintain the river's quality spring fly fishery by keeping big trout in the river, and it would also provide adequate water for the vast majority of steelhead redds. Although biologists hoped steelhead redds would have hatched out by the time water levels dropped, it seemed that some steelhead might be lost. Wightman said that the key to the Cowichan's productivity was in maintaining optimum flows over the summer, to sustain young fish. "This means that desiccation of a few steelhead redds in the spring [because of low water] will be of little consequence to the eventual smolt yield, as this is predominantly set by the amount of available living space during low summer flows."

≈

That biologists were giving life at the same time they were taking it away didn't sit well with Saysell, unofficial guardian of the Cowichan and untiring champion of its trout and steelhead.

"I can't believe the department of fisheries is doing this," he said one spring as we walked the river. "They seem to have total power. The resident trout fisherman is being left out of the equation while they manage for chinook."

It was May and the banks of the river seemed to be surging with life after lying still under the deep snows of winter. Saysell stood in his backyard looking at the river. A few weeks earlier his lawn had been underwater; a current had licked at his back deck, and he launched his drift boat from his driveway. But now the river was in retreat, pulling back across the lawn, dropping down the bank. Saysell walked across the soggy grass to where a row of sticks stood in a muddy strip along the river. Every day he walked out a little farther and shoved another stick into the muck. He was marking the rapid dewatering of the Cowichan. It had gone from 45 cm/s, to 28, to 13 in a few days.

"It seems pointless to bring the adult fish up in the fall if you're going to drop the river so fast in the spring that you trap the fry. It just doesn't make sense . . . When the water level drops it cuts them off like that," he says, bringing his right hand down like a guillotine. "They get stranded in little puddles."

A passionate and dedicated protector of steelhead, Wightman was stung by Saysell's criticism. He certainly didn't want to lose any steelhead redds. He was just doing his best to balance the needs of steelhead, trout fishermen, salmon and the forest industry. In a letter outlining the difficult challenges of flow regulation in the Cowichan, Wightman noted with some apparent frustration: "At the present time, there is simply not enough water to completely satisfy all user groups."

By 1990, Wightman, Tutty and other fisheries biologists had come to feel that the only solution to the annual water shortage was to raise the Cowichan Lake weir, so that more water could be held back for the fish. That would allow for greater flows in the spring, while retaining an adequate supply for the fall surges.

"There simply just isn't enough water for everyone under the present regime," said Tutty. "Every September we pray for rain. We shouldn't be praying for rain, we should be storing it. Our position is we'd like to see more storage for the fish . . . we're talking about feathering that dam up 10 inches for salmon."

If the weir is raised, it will probably be the first time in B.C. that a dam has been raised to help a fishery. Nobody has suggested the opposite approach — taking out the weir and returning the river to its natural rhythm. Not yet anyway. For one thing, the forest industry is the base of the local economy; for another, fisheries managers like the weir. If they can get a few more inches of water stored in the lake, they argue, they can bring the Cowichan back to a natural balance, while at the same time reducing the impact of any future droughts.

Saysell, who has fished the river for 30 years, and whose late father fished it long before that, is wary. He says he appreciates that the weir helps fish get through the hot summers, and he reluctantly agrees with Wightman and Tutty that raising the weir may be the only solution now. But he rejects any suggestion that the weir is an improvement on nature, and wonders why society so unquestioningly accepts that a river as important as the Cowichan should be managed first for industry and only second for fish.

"We had a remarkable river before the weir was there," he says. "Why don't we manage this river for the steelhead, trout and salmon? Why not turn this whole thing around and say to Fletcher Challenge, 'Look, this is how much water we need, you figure out how to make do with what's left.' Maybe then they'd learn to use less water."

Saysell appreciates the economic importance of the forest industry. For more than 20 years he's made his living as a faller, guiding on weekends. But he believes that in the long run, having a healthy river is what's important. His uncompromising attitude about the importance of fish habitat has earned him a lot of enemies in the small logging community.

"A lot of people don't like the stand I've taken on the river," he says. "My wife and I have lost a lot of friends. Now I carry a baseball bat behind my truck seat, just in case I need it."

He has been such a thorn in the side of the logging industry that Fletcher Challenge tried, in 1991, to have him fired, taking him through a five-step grievance process, claiming he wasn't productive enough as a faller. In the final hearing, the company admitted it had no case. Saysell was *more* productive than most fallers. The real problem was that, as long as he was in the woods, there was a whistle ready to be blown. When logging road erosion started to damage steelhead habitat in the Caycuse River, it was Saysell who called the Department of the Environment and alerted the media. When the woodworkers union, IWA-Canada, formed an environmental watchdog committee, Saysell was the motivating force. And when 300 loggers staged a protest outside Fletcher Challenge's Vancouver office tower, holding up pictures of unacceptable clearcut operations, Saysell was again largely to blame.

Saysell fished the Cowichan as a boy. He raised a family on its banks and today lives in a small house with his wife, Gail, just above the winter high-water mark. His father, Ron, was a guide before him and taught him the secrets of the river. When his father died, Saysell scattered his ashes in a favourite pool. As he sat there alone in the boat, thinking about life and death, watching the river take the ashes, a trout rose below him. He picked up his rod, cast and caught a big rainbow. Saysell seldom kills fish, but he saw that trout as a gift, so he took it home and had it mounted. It graces the wall of his den, and just below it is a stone carving of a brown trout, done by an artist who lives on the river. The statue was being carved when Joe's father died. One day the sculptor, Gus Galbraith, appeared on Joe's doorstep and said, "What do you think this is?" Joe looked at it and felt his heart murmur. "It's Ronnie," he said.

≈

The Cowichan is one of the world's best salmon and trout rivers, although it is relatively unknown. Once, before the time of the weir, it had a greater reputation. In the 1930s and 1940s, the Flyfishers Club of London regularly posted bulletins about the river for its members, as did the Theodore Gordon Flyfishers in its New York clubhouse. In those days the Cowichan was known as a pristine river, a near-perfect fishing stream that had prolific insect hatches and produced big trout, steelhead and salmon.

The Cowichan is still an incredible river, despite the intake pipe, the weir, conflicting demands over flow rates, intense fishing pressure and the impacts of heavy logging in the watershed.

The river may not be what it once was, but there are those who think that it could be.

Ted Burns stirs his coffee gently and speaks about the Cowichan as a great artist would speak of a half-finished masterpiece. His gaze is fixed at some point beyond the arborite table top. He can see the river. He knows what it could be. It could be full of salmon, trout and steelhead, self-perpetuating runs of wild fish that go on forever. He sees the habitat potential. He knows the Cowichan can be great again. It can be a river talked about in London and New York.

Burns, a freelance biologist, came to Lake Cowichan in 1983, looking for a place to establish a holistic approach to fisheries management. He fell in love with the river and the great lakehead watershed that fed it. This, he thought, is it. The Cowichan Lake Salmonid Enhancement Society hired him on the spot.

"I wanted a river that was large enough and interesting

enough, and interesting enough to other biologists so that what I did would be noticed," says Burns. "I looked at the river and saw what was, and what could be." Then he rolled up his sleeves and went to work.

One of the first things Burns did was organize a fry salvage program. For decades local people had intermittently worked to save salmon fry trapped in landlocked pools created when either the weir, or dry weather, reduced flows. Until Burns came along, however, nobody really did it in a serious, organized manner.

Burns began studying the small streams feeding into the lake and river. He walked them, got to know the pools, peered under rocks and cutbanks. He watched the way the weather affected them; saw them shrink in the sunlight. Pretty soon he began to understand the sequential way in which the streams ran dry. He could predict the progression and, armed with a dip net and a bucket, stay a step ahead of nature.

Before Burns came along the expected survival rate of salmon fry in the Cowichan tributary streams was about 8 percent. That is, for every 100 salmon eggs that hatched, 92 would die before they migrated down to the lake or the big river.

Now, working with a few volunteer helpers, Burns has bumped the survival rate to up to 30 percent. He saves between 200,000 and 300,000 fry a year; 80 percent coho and 20 percent trout. He finds his fish in small pools that are growing smaller by the day, and traps them in a Marquesette net, a fine-mesh fabric stretched between two long broom handles.

"We've had up to 15,000 in a net," he says as he prepares to wade through a pool. A wave carrying leaf matter, twigs, and green algae washes out the end of the pool ahead of him and seeps into the gravel. A single silver coho spills out and wriggles on the damp pebbles. Burns comes back for it after he shakes 22 similar fry out of his net into a bucket of water. He holds the tiny fish in his palm for a moment, wondering at its delicate colours. "They are the most beautiful of all the fry," he says. Coho have a distinct white flag on their anal fin, and touches of burnt orange.

Burns has studied thousands of them, and he's noticed something: "There's two types. There's a type programmed to go to a lake — they're round, cylindrical with thin fins. Then there's the stream coho. The stream fish are deeper, laterally compressed, very colourful, with large fins adapted to fast water, as opposed to the lake."

We are walking up a streambed that is two lanes wide. In the fall there will be a traffic jam of spawning coho here, but at the moment it's an empty gravel road through the forest, with a string of pools connected by a trickle of water that sometimes vanishes underground.

"The streams dry up to dust," says Burns. "Eventually there is nothing. When they get down to pools or just the trickle between pools, that's when we hit them." If they weren't salvaged by Burns and his volunteer helpers, the fish would eventually suffocate in the pools, or they'd fall prey to an endless array of predators that stalk the dwindling streams.

"Everything knows," says Burns, pausing in the shade of a maple. Birds sing in the forest. "You'd be amazed what preys on them — robins, starlings, snakes. Everything. We even have the raccoons coming, digging the eggs out before they hatch. As soon as the fry emerge, every bird is waiting for them."

There are bigger problems than that. Walking upstream we find skidder tracks 40 centimetres deep in the dry streambed. The ground is littered with shattered tree trunks, and it is torn and rutted where heavy equipment dragged away trees.

The valley has been intensely logged over the last 50 years and is now mostly second growth, except for pockets of old timber. One stream at a time, logging has taken a toll, destabilizing flow regimes and increasing erosion and sedimentation. On the nearby Chemainus River, for example, fisheries biologists noted a "drastic reduction" in salmon numbers that coincided directly with extensive logging. On that river alone, stocks declined from 60,000 chum, 4350 coho and 2480 steelhead to 9350 chum, 348 coho and 453 steelhead. Biologists attributed the decline directly to the impact of logging.

Burns was now looking at a small-scale manifestation of a much bigger problem. "Look at those skidder tracks," he said in disbelief. "How do they expect salmon to spawn here? They just trashed it."

The West Branch of the Robertson Side Channel, as the creek is known, runs through private land. Whoever logged it may have simply been exercising their rights as land owners. But they did not consider the rights of salmon.

"They came in here in the winter when the ground was as soft as loon shit," says a disgusted Burns. "Look at this. Good gracious. This is definitely fish habitat. There's no debate about that."

It *was* fish habitat. Now it's a jumbled mess of gravel, mud and broken trees.

Burns stands and looks at the destruction, shaking his head. Hundreds of metres of streambed have been destroyed, and silt from the ripped-up streambank will drift down, later that fall, to cover spawning beds below. There is nothing he can do now. He takes his net and bucket, and starts down. Pool by pool he scoops out tiny salmon fry, saving them from robins, skidders and the heat of the sun. He will carry them to deeper water: to pools that won't run dry or to the big lake.

"We've got about 15,000 from this stream so far this year," says Burns proudly. But that's nothing compared to what they save in pools along the Cowichan. "Some people got 90,000 from one pool one year. Imagine that," he says.

Burns will make three or four trips to the creek each spring, and he'll run his net through each pool three or four times on every visit.

"We've tried everything," he says. "This is the best way."

The stream had only a handful of spawners a few years ago, but last fall 300 coho came back. To Burns it was compelling evidence that his low-tech, labour-intensive approach was working.

His holistic plan to save the Cowichan focuses on cheap, simple techniques and is heavy on community involvement. He usually has a volunteer or two working with him when he walks the streams, and sometimes at night his phone will ring and a voice will say: "You better get in there, boy, that creek is going fast!" Hunters, dirt bikers, bird watchers, loggers — they all call Burns when they come across a stream that's starting to wither.

"I think that's the future of fisheries — a lot of little things that are low impact by themselves, but if you do them together they add up. Things that can be done by ordinary people. If you're going to see optimum fisheries management it has to be based on community involvement."

The village of Lake Cowichan has embraced his approach. Even the beavers are joining in. Burns pulls his pickup truck off the Cowichan Lake Road, then leads me along a path beside a tiny trickle of water. Eventually we reach the source — a beaver pond. Beaver Creek, which empties into Cowichan River just below Cowichan Lake, was once an important salmon producer, but after the area was logged, the beaver left and the creek soon ran out of water.

"It dried up. Turned into a skunk cabbage patch," says Burns, looking out over a large dark pond nestled in the woods. "The beaver got in there, raised the level and made it almost to perfect design."

Leo Nelson and other volunteers worked with Burns to dig out the old streambed. They filled 2000 metres of it with gravel and stones. With much difficulty, a pipe was sunk under the base of the beaver dam so that water could be released slowly in the summer, to keep salmon fry alive.

Before Burns, the beaver, and the people of Lake Cowichan went to work on it, Beaver Creek had about 10 salmon a year spawning in it. It was basically hard tack and skunk cabbage, and the fish that spawned did so in desperation.

Last fall 600 coho came to Beaver Creek. They spawned in clean gravel under the shade of tall, second-growth timber.

Burns and Nelson watched the stream fill up with salmon and it made them feel better than you could believe.

"We built this stream," said Burns, smiling. From where we stood on the bank we could see coho fry holding in the shade of a drooping fern, their white flags waving in the steady current.

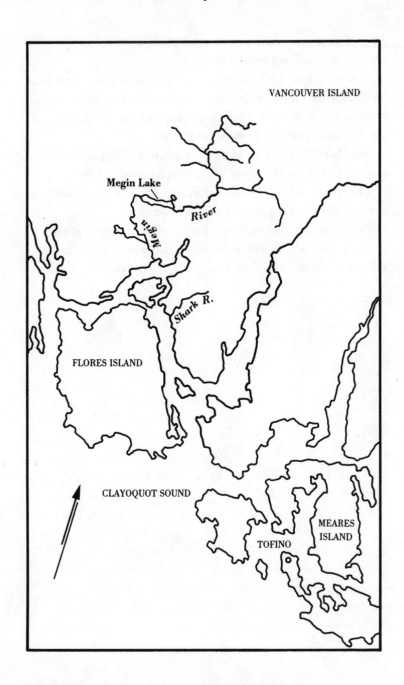

THE WAY THE
WORLD WAS

The Megin

It's raining inside the plane. Drops of water fall from the top of the windscreen onto my notebook. Streams run along the side window. The prop on the single-engine Beaver blows the rain back against the cabin with such force that it turns into strands of mercury, filters through the superstructure and splatters across my lap. This isn't a problem. A few minutes ago I was out there in the full force of the rain, waiting on a windswept beach for the Beaver to come in on its ponderous floats. Even in July it can be cool on the ocean, in the Pacific Northwest's temperate zone. Over my clothes I wear a tightly woven canvas jacket known as a Bonedry, and Helly-Hansen rainpants made of green rubber with a fabric backing — sealed against the elements except for the dampness spreading down the back of my collar. You just can't keep *all* the rain out. The pilot hands me a paper towel to wipe my notebook. Ink smears across the page.

I am looking out at a world drenched with precipitation, where downpours of 160 millimetres a day are common. Rain falls on the sea with fury, giving the green waters a silver sheen.

We pass over Easter Lake, sombre and uninviting, and look down Sydney Inlet, a deep fjord on Clayoquot (pronounced "Klaquit") Sound, north of the small town of Tofino on Vancouver Island's western shore. Rain mist is everywhere. It clings to the forest, creeps across the sea, reaches in long tendrils down the inlets, buries the off-shore islands and shrouds the steep mountains. Wherever the fog lifts you can see a silent green carpet spreading to the distance. This is the greatest remaining temperate rainforest on earth — and it is rapidly being liquidated.

In a 1991 paper for Conservation International, consultant Keith Moore reported that temperate rainforests still occur in Chile, Norway, Australia, New Zealand and on the northwest coast of North America, covering no more than 30 million hectares or about 2.5 percent of the area occupied by tropical rainforests. "About two thirds of the world's temperate rainforest is on the northwest coast of North America," he wrote. "These forests are overwhelmingly coniferous. They represent the largest organic accumulations of any ecosystems that exist in the world. They include approximately 25 tree species and up to 350 species of birds and mammals. Some researchers have recently claimed that if the soil organisms in the below ground ecosystems in these forests are included, they may be as rich in biological diversity as the tropical rainforest."

The temperate rainforest covers the entire coastline of British Columbia, reaching up coastal inlets and river valleys for 150 kilometres. It is about 6 million hectares, which sounds like a lot until you realize twice that much has already been cut and what's left is being logged at 40,000 hectares a year.

All the economically accessible old-growth forest in British Columbia will be gone in 15 years at current harvesting rates. The great blanket that covers the outer coast of Vancouver Island is a dwindling remnant of what it once was, and may have already reached the minimal size at which an entire ecosystem can be preserved. As logging progresses, the forest is being divided into increasingly isolated islands. The forest blocks left at Kyuquot/Brooks Peninsula and Clayoquot are surrounded by growing clearcuts.

Most of the ancient forest is found in remote regions beyond the end of the provincial highway system, which means its destruction has been witnessed by a relatively small number of people. As the 1990s began, most British Columbians were unaware that the last great, ancient rainforests on the coast would soon be gone. Only a handful of protesters — members of the Western Canada Wilderness Committee, the Sierra Club, the Heritage Forests Society, Friends of Clayoquot Sound, and individuals — stood in the way of logging. Some were jailed for defying court injunctions and blocking logging roads. They were largely ridiculed or ignored by the mass media. Some were threatened with beatings or death by people who accused them of economic sabotage and of having an insatiable desire to preserve wilderness. Those who fought to save the rainforest ecosystem simply did what they could. For most of them, becoming activists was not a choice. Once they had walked through a grove of ancient trees they were committed.

The temperate rainforest on British Columbia's rain-soaked coast holds Western hemlock, Douglas fir, Pacific silver fir and Sitka spruce so tall they would reach above most of Vancouver's highrises if they grew in the city. One tree, named the Carmanah Giant when it was discovered in 1988, is taller than the Peace Tower on Parliament Hill. There are also yellow and red cedars in the forest — trees so thick that two people can't link hands around them. Spread your hands and lean against a tree like that. Think about its age. It is 700 years old at least, perhaps 1000. It was huge when Juan Perez of the Spanish navy brought his ship *Santiago* to anchor near Tofino, off Estevan Point, becoming the first European to sight the coast of British Columbia.

That was in 1774. Perez is history, but the tree is still there, standing in a forest that has taken 12,000 years to reach its climax stage. Look up until you are dizzy. Inhale and let the smell of its bark fill your lungs. Feel how soft and sweet the air is, as you breathe in what the forest breathes out. Look at the way it turns the light a golden green colour as it filters through the massive canopy. Listen to rain drops falling from boughs 100 metres above you, ringing as they break on the nodding heads of deer fern, or strike a thick carpet of sphagnum moss. Imagine, if you can, cutting this giant down. Lining it up so it will fall between the other huge trees. Hoping it won't explode. When it's done, after it has fallen with a roar, its branches flailing as if in a violent storm, its trunk rocking on the ground like a bull elephant dropped with a shot to the chest, after that, move on and cut another. Keep going through the whole valley. Take all the trees down — the 1000-year-old elders, the 50-year-old new growth. Start along the valley floor where the flood waters of some pristine, crystal river like Carmanah, or Shark or Megin, has moved sediment up onto the banks, replenishing the soil's nutrients and growing some of the biggest trees on the planet. Move up from the river and clear the slopes. Cut the steep grades where the trees fall with such force that many of them shatter on impact. Leave that as waste. Keep going. Sweating. Hauling your chain saw. Looking back to the deep cuts into the earth left by the backhoes and Cats as they slice logging roads back and forth up the hillside. Listen for the sound of dynamite as the land is broken open to create flats for camps and log sorting grounds. Strip the forest from the crest of the mountain to the sea shore. It is known as clearcutting, and for 100 years that has been the way the logging industry has done business in B.C., justifying it with economic imperative.

Foresters say clearcutting is the safest, most cost-effective way to log. Environmental impact, they say, is fleeting. In a few years the clearcuts, brown and red and black, will start to green up. Small birds will flit through the waist-high foliage, looking for seeds. Deer will come out to nibble tender plants. Eagles will look elsewhere for nests. The streams will get a little dirty for a while, but the fish will do fine. Logging doesn't hurt water quality much. After a few years, they say, it will all look great. And in 60 to 70 years, they will come back and do it again. This is sustained, sustainable development, they say. In the meantime, enjoy. Industry calls it "sharing the forest."

≈

It is all a lie of course. Clearcut logging has devastating impact. It must be understood that you can have immensely profitable logging, or you can have birds, wildlife and wilderness. You cannot have both at the same time. You cannot, despite the industry line, have it all. After clearcutting, many birds, including the rare marbled murrelet, will simply vanish; in winter, when the snows are deep, the black-tailed deer won't find the lichens they used to get below the ancient trees. The ungulate population will drop. The wolves and cougars will follow. Black bears, which typically den in old, hollow trees, will wander like wild dogs across the stripped landscape.

The forest industry, which spends millions of dollars a year on campaigns portraying loggers as harvesters of the land, has not yet been able to figure out how to clearcut a watershed without severely affecting the entire hydrology of a valley. After trees are cut, their massive root networks die. Steep slopes become more prone to slides and torrents. Logging road construction, which became better in the environmentally conscious '90s, still creates massive erosion. Gravel spawning beds fill with suffocating silt. The crevasses between boulders are choked by shifting substrate, paving the riverbed, and depriving fry of overwintering shelter. The clear water turns brown whenever it rains, carrying what scientists call suspended solids. The silt impairs the respiratory

functions of fish and they become so stressed that increased con-
centrations of plasma cortisol, which suppresses the immune
system, can be measured in the blood. The fish are more susceptible to bacterial pathogens and, among other things, their fins
may begin to rot.

Settling in the spawning gravel, where water pushes oxygen
down to the eggs, suspended solids fall with killing silence.
Fewer than half of trout and salmon embryos emerge from river-
beds when the spawning gravel contains 30 to 40 percent silt. At
Jim Creek, in Montana, scientists with the U.S. Forest Service,
Montana Department of Fish, Wildlife and Parks, and Water
Quality Bureau, did a study specifically to measure the impact of
suspended solids on fish eggs. They sampled the gravel and
monitored the trout population above and below a timber sale
area, prior to and after logging, from 1988 to 1990. They found
the average percentage of silt in gravel above the logging area
did not change. However, below logging, the percentage of fine
material in the gravel increased to 50 percent. Cutthroat trout
eggs in gravel with 40 percent fine material have a mortality of
75 percent. When the fine material level increases to 50 percent,
as it did in Jim Creek, the mortality rate hits 96 percent.

The study's conclusion: "The fisheries habitat . . . has signifi-
cantly deteriorated below the West Jim Timber Sale since recent
land management activity by Plum Creek Timberlands. Based on
predicted embryo survival, bull trout, a species of special concern
in Montana, will experience 100 percent mortality in sampled
spawning areas. Westslope cutthroat trout, also a species of special concern, may experience extremely low survival (4 percent)
if spawning occurs in areas sampled downstream of the sale."
The scientists found that, after logging, there weren't any fish in
Jim Creek below the cut, but they could still find them in the
undisturbed water above.

The forest industry claims clearcut logging does not seriously affect fish populations, and it has argued against leaving swaths of trees, known as green strips, along valley bottoms. Fisheries biologists fight for the retention of green strips, stating that streamside vegetation provides cooling shade for fish in summer and a long-term supply of organic debris, which is important in winter. Let's agree on this at least: a narrow green strip really doesn't do much good if the mountains above are bare, so if clearcutting is allowed, it may as well take it all, including the last big trees along the riverbanks. It would be decent at such times, however, to acknowledge the death that is being caused and issue a prayer for forgiveness.

Not far from the last stronghold of the ancient temperate rainforests on Clayoquot Sound, MacMillan Bloedel Ltd. logged the Cameron River watershed. The Cameron River is known to tourists who drive Highway 4 across the Island to the west coast, because they cross it in Cathedral Grove, a forest park outside Port Alberni. MacMillan Bloedel left the grove of huge trees along the highway as a testament to the great rainforests that once blanketed the area. Every year thousands of tourists stop their cars and wander through the pocket of trees, marvelling at their size and profound beauty. The Cameron River chatters innocently in its bed. Upstream, where tourists don't venture, clearcutting has removed the forest and the river has a different sound to it. If a river ever howled, this one did.

Logging began in Cameron Valley in the mid-1960s, concentrating at first in the upper watershed which is characterized by relatively shallow, stable soils, and unstable, steep gullies. The big problems started in the gullies. In 1986 the Department of Fisheries and Oceans went into the Cameron watershed to do a stream survey because suspended solids were washing down through Cathedral Grove. Much of the material was so fine that it drifted across Cameron Lake, rather than settling out, and went down the Little Qualicum River where it was affecting the

operations of a federal salmon hatchery. On January 17 and 18
that year, heavy rains fell on a deep snow pack in the Cameron
Valley, which was denuded of forest cover. A debris torrent
started on a major tributary; two logged areas (settings #514 and
#410) were soon covered by two metres of running water. The
mainline bridge over Cop Creek was blown out after muck and
logging debris collected around the structure, and water built up
behind it. That winter a massive collection of wood waste,
sluiced off the slopes by the rain and melting snow, had been deposited across the mainstem of the Cameron River. The jam,
with a surface area exceeding 6000 square metres, diverted almost the entire flow of the Cameron, causing massive erosion.
DFO experts estimated 20,000 square metres of floodplain soils
were washed into the river at that one spot alone. When the
bridge jam on Cop Creek blew out, another 1500 cubic metres
of gravel/rock material was released into the river.

The logging road system became a series of streams, directing
run-off into gullies where more erosion took place, discharging
200,000 cubic metres of sediment, mostly fine morainal material
and organics. "These gullies are evident on earlier air photos,"
wrote DFO researchers, "however, fresh and massive erosion is
evident throughout the gulley complex." Whole hillsides were being moved into the river.

DFO reported that "masses of logging slash" had entered the
stream directly from clearcuts. No charges were levelled against
MacMillan Bloedel. The Department of Fisheries, which since 1977
has had the power, under the Fisheries Act, to fine companies for
any work "that results in the harmful alteration, disruption or destruction of fish habitat," thought it better to cooperate with
industry. It recommended that terracing, grass seeding and other
methods be tried to stabilize the slopes, and that log jams be
cleared to return the river to its original bed. I think: grass seeds
to replace the root network of an ancient forest?

≅

Much of the Alaskan temperate rainforest is scrub and only about 250,000 hectares is high quality timber; 7000 hectares a year is logged.

In the Douglas fir region of western Washington and Oregon, about 1 million hectares of old growth forest remain from an original 6 million. It is being logged at a rate of about 28,000 hectares a year.

In California, virtually none of the original 1.7 million hectares of rainforest exist today. There are no entirely unlogged watersheds of any size in the Golden State.

In B.C., the temperate rainforest zone covers most of Vancouver Island, the Queen Charlotte Islands and the west side of the Coast Mountains. In 1890 it was virtually untouched. By 1990 it was on its last legs. What will be lost once it's gone?

"This biogeoclimatic zone has a greater biodiversity than any other biogeoclimatic zone in B.C., including the greatest diversity of wildlife, birds, amphibians and reptiles," states Conservation International. "Since B.C. has more species of birds and mammals and greater diversity than any other province, the temperate rainforest has the greatest biodiversity in Canada.

"At present approximately 40,000 hectares are being clearcut annually in the coastal forest and harvest is widely distributed along the entire range of temperate rainforest. Much of the remaining forest [is] under a variety of long term tenure arrangements, either Tree Farm Licenses or Forest Licenses, to large forest companies, who are responsible for the most important management decisions about these forests. Present harvesting rates are predicted upon the assumption that all the remaining old growth forest, outside of protected areas, will be harvested."

On the map it may seem as if a large area of rainforest remains, but logging activities during the last century have reached to almost every corner on the coast. Few big tracts survive. Fewer still are the number of intact watersheds that have ancient rainforests from the mountains to the sea.

Reported Conservation International: "On the east coast of Vancouver Island, all 28 watersheds greater than 5000 hectares have been logged to some degree. There are no remaining unlogged watersheds at all. Logging began in the last unlogged watershed on the east coast of the Island, the Shushartie, about a year ago with no attention paid by any agency or environmental group.

"There are also no entire unlogged watersheds that are protected. Three tributaries of the Campbell River system are protected in Strathcona Park but the Campbell has been dammed, heavily logged and polluted by mining.

"On the west coast of Vancouver Island, the situation is only slightly better. One significant watershed, the 18,000 hectare Moyeha, is unlogged and protected in Strathcona Park. It is the only entire, unlogged watershed in excess of 5000 hectares on Vancouver Island or the mainland coast of British Columbia that is fully protected . . .

"Only 1 of the 13 watersheds in excess of 20,000 hectares on the west coast of the Island is unlogged. This is the 24,000 hectare Megin, adjacent to the Moyeha in Clayoquot Sound . . .

"In summary, on Vancouver Island there are 27 watersheds greater than 20,000 hectares. *Only one, the Megin, is unlogged and none are protected.*"

Until Conservation International did the study, no summary of the status of British Columbia's remaining temperate rainforest existed. The B.C. Ministry of Forests subsequently launched an Old Growth Strategy Project, to start officially identifying critical old-growth areas that might need to be placed "under short term deferral," and to start working on a long term framework for old-growth reserves. Until 1990 the ministry had never really acknowledged that ancient rainforests had a value beyond the worth of the lumber they contained. Does the old-growth strategy indicate the B.C. Forest Service will save some significant stands of temperate rainforest? With only a handful of watersheds left unlogged on Vancouver Island, the ministry will have to act decisively and it will have to act *against* the best interests of the forest industry — which is highly unlikely. History suggests that the forest industry itself will offer distractions and false compromises while striving to log the last few untouched watersheds on Vancouver Island. As the remaining watersheds are remote, chances are that most people will never know what was lost.

≅

We awake before dawn on a gravel bar of the Megin. Over the sound of the river my brother Timothy and I hear a series of loud, high, kree notes calling us from our tent. Looking up to the sky we see small birds with mottled breasts and fast wing beats circling above Megin Lake. They are marbled murrelets. There are about a dozen of them, flying in from the great forested hills, calling to each other, circling, then heading off in pairs down the valley towards the ocean to feed. Somewhere out there in the forest, high in the great trees, the rare birds have settled their nests in huge balls of moss. It wasn't until 1990 that the first marbled murrelet nest was found in British Columbia, in a towering spruce in Carmanah Valley.

The nesting habits of marbled murrelets, which are now threatened because of old-growth logging, were one of the biggest mysteries in the bird world for decades. Early ornithological papers carried titles like "The Mystery of the Marbled Murrelet" and "Enigma of the Pacific."

The first nest found in North America was discovered in 1974 by Hoyt Foster, a tree surgeon who was cutting damaged limbs from a huge Douglas fir in a campground in Big Basin Red-

woods State Park, in California's Santa Cruz Mountains. The
nest, which had apparently been used for years, consisted simply
of a depression in the bright green moss covering the limbs of
the old-growth tree.

In the spring of 1991, speaking in defence of logging the Walbran Valley on Vancouver Island, then-forests minister Claude
Richmond issued a press release stating, "Timber harvesting . . .
will not adversely affect the marbled murrelet."

He based this reassurance on information that the murrelet
nest discovered in Carmanah a year earlier had not been used
since. That proved to him that murrelets used different areas
each year, and could simply move if their nesting trees were cut
down. A comforting theory, but one not supported by scientific
observation.

According to the International Council for Bird Preservation,
the destruction of old-growth forest is the greatest threat to the
continued existence of marbled murrelets.

In a paper published in *American Birds*, 1988, the Audubon
Society of Portland, Oregon, stated: "Lack of knowledge in itself
is a threat to the species. Considering that as few as 10 to 50
years remain before most old-growth habitat is eliminated (according to existing plans) within 75 kilometres of the coasts of
Washington, Oregon, and California, immediate needs are to
protect nesting areas . . . The role forests play in winter for activities other than nesting is also unknown and must be
determined. It must be determined if birds displaced by habitat
loss use replacement habitat, and what impact continued frag-
mentation of old-growth forests has on the population.

"Such information is essential before adequate protection can
take place in light of pressures to remove old-growth and mature
timber . . . Considering the complex biology of the bird, its cre-
puscular nature inland, and the fact that in the Pacific
Northwest it apparently nests high in trees located in forests hav-

ing the greatest biomass of any in the temperate world, we have before us a major research challenge which far exceeds the Spotted Owl."

In January 1988, the National Audubon Society, the Oregon Natural Resources Council and over 40 chapters of the National Audubon Society in Washington, Oregon and northern California submitted a petition to the U.S. Fish and Wildlife Service to list the marbled murrelet as a threatened species.

In 1989, MacMillan Bloedel made ready to log Carmanah Valley by sending a biologist in to assess the region's biodiversity. According to a report submitted by D.F. Bendickson, Registered Professional Forester and divisional engineer for the company, one of the key objectives was "to determine the species, distribution and approximate number of waterfowl using the watershed."

Bendickson's report to the B.C. Forest Service states: "No waterfowl were observed on any of the spring or fall helicopter flights. The watershed receives some local use by common mergansers . . . logging is not expected to adversely affect the present population."

MacMillan Bloedel researchers, whizzing through the valley in a Bell Jet Ranger at a cruising speed of 95 kilometres an hour, saw no marbled murrelets.

"Based on these results, no constraints are recommended on the development and harvesting of timber."

Later that year, using a research platform built high in the forest canopy by environmentalists, the Canadian Wildlife Service confirmed a relatively large population of murrelets was using the valley.

The B.C. government, which would later yield to public pressure and create Carmanah Pacific Provincial Park in the lower valley, responded to the find by ordering the Western Canada Wilderness Committee to remove the platform. Richmond, the enlightened murrelet expert, said the platform, built by mountaineers 40 metres up a tree, was posing "a substantial degree of risk." His orders were ignored. Researchers later used the platform to watch murrelets — eventually tracking one to its nest.

≈

Next to Carmanah lies the Walbran, which Richmond said could be logged without adverse effect on marbled murrelets. His proposal: leave green strips along the river bottom, and intermittent strips from the river to the height of land. The patchwork threads of timber should be adequate to save the birds and other wild creatures, he argued.

There is no scientific proof that wildlife can survive given such marginal habitat. And there is little hope that even those small strips of green will be protected by the Ministry of Forests, which oversees cutting regulations.

Just south of Walbran lies the Loup Creek watershed. Western Forest Industries logged off part of the area in the 1970s, and other logging interests returned to the area in 1991.

That spring, John R. Stephen, a fishery officer in Sooke, wrote to the Ministry of Forests to raise concerns about Loup Creek.

His biggest worry was that, given the record, the ministry would not enforce the terms of cutting permits.

"W.F.I.'s work in Loup Creek is generally regarded as one of the worst examples of habitat logging damage in T.F.L. 46, and falls far short of inspiring confidence within environmental protection agencies that M.O.F. will increase its monitoring and enforcement of harvest standards over future logging in this drainage. There is little persuasive evidence indicating M.O.F. is willing or even able to correct its policy towards enforcement of the terms and conditions of Cutting Permits particularly with such notable lack of field staff.

"It is regrettable that logging which has resulted in widespread loss of fish habitat and forest land was ever permitted by M.O.F., but for the ministry to allow such practices to persist, most of which contravene M.O.F.'s own regulations, is difficult to accept.

"Culverts are undersized and unmaintained, ditches are plugged, old roads are collapsing, seasonal stream gullies are debris clogged, sidecasting continues, and steep, unstable slopes are being clearcut."

The problems outlined by Stephen can be found almost anywhere on the B.C. coast. Every time there's a heavy rainstorm, the environmental impact of such awful logging is highlighted. And every winter, when the Hawaiian high and Aleutian low pressure areas meet over the Pacific, heavy rainstorms are pushed on to the coast. The heaviest rains fall from Kyuquot Sound to Carmanah.

A typical winter storm reached the coast in early November 1989, creating widespread destruction that was directly linked to logging. In Tofino, from the seventh to the ninth, 198 millimetres of rain fell. During the same time Carmanah Point got 188 millimetres and Bamfield 216 millimetres. Soil on slopes exposed by clearcutting began to liquefy.

Everybody knew it was raining hard that week, but an indication that the storm was causing major damage came on Wednesday, the eighth, when people in Kyuquot, a heavily logged area on the north coast of the Island, saw Walters Cove turn "an opaque brown." The Kyuquot Economic and Environmental Protection Society (KEEPS) reported that by November 9, water travel in the area was hazardous because of debris washed out of the Artlish River valley.

Stan Kujala, of the prawn boat *Beroy*, said he was "appalled" by the damage, which he blamed on logging up the Artlish. He said there were "massive logs, deadheads, sticks and other debris" covering the usually clear waters of the bay.

"My prawn traps had been set in 30 fathoms of water. When we picked them up they were in 70 fathoms with both buoys sinking. We almost lost them due to the flooding and logs coming out of the river. The traps were covered in silt and had no prawns. Prior to this the fishing was excellent but due to the clearcut logging I don't expect to catch prawns here for years to come."

Kujala also had nets near where the Tahsish River pours into the Pacific. The Tahsish has not been extensively logged, with cutting limited to the upper valley only. The traps there were clean and free of silt. He caught prawns, despite the storm.

KEEPS reported that on November 10, "what sounded like jet planes filled the air over Kyuquot." A huge landslide had been unleashed on St. Paul's Dome, a clearcut mountain overlooking the cove.

"The noon slide was so large that, in spite of all the rain, the dust took a half-hour to settle . . . The rubble base of this slide is now estimated to be 500 metres (1/4 mile) across."

In Quatsino that week, commercial fisherman Jim Botel felt the impact of the storm when he was jolted out of bed at 4:30 a.m. A mountain slope above his waterfront home, logged 25 years earlier, suddenly let loose.

"The first warning I got was flying down the hill in the house. The roof came off and went flying over my head," he recalled. Botel said a neighbor's house was also destroyed by the slide, "and the only reason he got out alive was because he could see a candle burning in another house — it was so dark and with the rain lashing down you couldn't tell which way was up."

Darcy Yule, operations manager for the B.C. Forest Service in Campbell River, said there were slides in unlogged areas — but fully 90 percent of the slides that week were in areas where clearcutting had taken place. The main cause of slides, he said, was not logging itself, but old logging roads, which had destabilized slopes. He said new roads are built to much higher standards.

I figure if we give them 25 years, we'll see the same things happening all over again on the "new improved" road systems.

It seems pretty obvious that if we want to have marbled murrelets, and if we want to have rivers with wild stocks of fish in them, if we want complete, natural ecosystems, some of the last wilderness watersheds on the coast will have to be saved in their entirety. And, yes, some areas will have to be cut to preserve jobs, but in deciding what to take and what to leave, there should be no delusions about what it means.

≈

Steve Lawson's seven-metre, steel-hulled boat cuts across the blue waters of Clayoquot Sound pushed by twin 50 horsepower motors. For more than 15 years he's lived near the water, in a log house perched on a rocky cliff on Wickanninish Island. He and his wife, Susanne Hare, built the house with their own hands using timber salvaged from the beaches. The logs had drifted free from booms being towed along the coast by forest company tugs. Outside his back door are 1000-year-old spruce trees that cloak the small, privately owned island. It is one place that will never be logged, but few other areas are protected. Once the mountains of Clayoquot Sound were covered with ancient forests, but today there are huge open swathes appearing where logging companies have clearcut entire mountainsides. Much of the richest timber is in the valley bottoms. Many have been logged right to the borders of salmon streams and, in other places, from mountain peaks to ocean front. The clearcuts expose a sea of stumps and logging waste. Whatever the loggers say in defence of their profession, there is always something like this to remind us of the truth.

To Lawson, who runs a charter boat when he's not involved in environmental protests, there is no excuse for stripping the earth in this way. To him, what is happening to the hills of Clayoquot Sound is a crime against nature. Some regard him as a criminal. Both he and his wife have been jailed for blockading logging roads.

Lawson throttles back to an idle as the logging road scarring the hillside above Sulphur Pass comes into sight. Fletcher Challenge voluntarily abandoned the road in the face of protests from Lawson and others, but the company still holds cutting rights. The road deadends in the forest. Nearby is a MacMillan Bloedel clearcut and, in another direction, a cleared mountain with a stark, bristling stand of timber left along one ridge like a Mohawk haircut.

"We used to come down here in the autumn, before logging started, and the whole area — as far as you could see — was full of jumping salmon. Now it's pathetic. Maybe five percent of the salmon are left. It's just gone," he says.

Lawson points out the kind of logging he thinks caused the disappearance of the salmon. The valley has been clearcut. Raw, brown mountainsides slope to the river. "There used to be giant spruce in there. That was the first thing they took. Then they took the rest."

Lawson heads his boat to an inlet at the head of the nearby Moyeha River, the only unlogged watershed on Vancouver Island that is completely protected, being surrounded by Strathcona Park.

"This is what it used to be like," he says, striding through the tall grass on the tidal flats. Hanging from the spruce are long beards of yellow lichen that doesn't grow on trees until they are 100 years old. It is this lichen that sustains deer populations during times of deep snow. When the trees are gone, the lichen is gone for a century. The deer are decimated.

There are trout and steelhead in the river, says Lawson, as he closely watches his two daughters, Misty, 6, and Cosy, 9. "You don't lose sight of your kids in this country," he says. "There are cougars."

Later Cosy cautions a visitor, saying: "A cougar had my friend for lunch." She's talking about the death of a 12-year-old boy who was killed while walking alone on the beach below nearby Cat Face Mountain.

Lawson was visited by a cougar on Wickanninish Island once. It swam out to hunt for deer. He saw the tracks near his house and for three weeks carried a shotgun. One day he felt a chill down his spine. "I knew the cougar was there and I looked and looked," he says. "Just when I was about to turn away I saw his face in the bush. He was crouched about three metres away. I put a shell in the chamber and, for a moment, I thought I'd just shoot him from the hip. I'm pretty good at that. But then I thought about the kids and about having a wounded cougar on the island. So I brought the gun up, ever so slowly, and between the time the stock passed my chest and reached my shoulder, he vanished."

Lawson let out a roar and fired a shot into the tree trunk — a territorial declaration the cougar seemed to accept. It left the island. Lawson tells his story about the cougar with a certain sense of respect and wonder. He accepts cougars for being the predators they are. The world of nature, he believes, was not meant to be controlled by humans completely. Without the forests the deer will vanish and so too will the cougars. Lawson's kids would be safe from cats then — yet he would never see it that way. What he fears more than cougars is a world in which his daughters have to grow up without great forests surrounding them.

We get back in the boat and turn down another inlet, coming to rest on a beach where the stones are covered with yellow seaweed. Lawson gets out and leads the way through the trees, following a small stream. We climb a steep pinnacle and look down into a black plunge pool under a 30-metre waterfall. At high tide, saltwater backs up into the pool, and Lawson says native legend holds that basking sharks come here to sleep in the oxygen-rich water beneath the falls. The stream is called Shark River. Its headwaters are due to be logged — and no one knows how that will affect the sharks.

"If we could get a picture of a shark sleeping in this pool we'd be able to stop logging," says Lawson. But so far, nobody's been able to get such a picture. The government's plan is to log, and worry about the sharks later. And if no one ever sees another shark in the plunge pool, that will be taken as proof they never used it. Or that, as in the Ministry of Forests' version of the marbled murrelets, they just moved on to new habitat.

It seems we are faced with only one of two choices: save what we have left of the natural world and try to learn from it, or destroy it and hope for the best.

≅

Going up through the canyon of the Megin River, my brother and I could touch stone walls on both sides of the canoe at once. Beneath us the water was golden green, the colour and clarity of sunlight filtered through a forest canopy.

There are pools on the river where the bottom is solid granite, washed clean of any sediment or gravel; there are pools where a million stones shine, each with its own shade of gray, green, white, black or red. There are deer tracks on the sandbars and blue huckleberries growing along the banks.

Hiking up in the forest you pass under huge standing giants and see the rotting bodies of cedars from which new growth is sprouting. There are boulders covered with moss as thick as a mattress. There is bear spoor, purple and flecked with berry seeds, and waterfalls that spill down cliffs with hanging fern gardens dripping in the sunlight.

Midway from the canyon to the sea, Megin Lake opens in the steep hills. The water warms there, and salmon fry school in the bays, followed by hungry cutthroat trout.

Below the lake, band-tailed pigeons scatter with a clap of wings above the drifting canoe. Blue grouse drum in the undergrowth, and varied thrush sing everywhere. In an eddy, a dozen trout, the white gape of their mouths showing, chase salmon fry, leaving a froth of drifting bubbles on the surface as they strike.

The river embraces you. Even in a cold rain its beauty is resonant.

We drift down to the sea, passing through a stone gateway into Shelter Inlet, where the ocean swell seems big and brawling after the gentle Megin. Waiting for hours, leaning against a rock outcrop that barely shelters us from the rain, we watch a gray loon. It surfaces with a silver fish in its beak, turns it with a toss of its head, swallows and dives again. It is completely at peace with the rain, like the forest.

When the float plane comes in, we paddle out through the chop and hold a pontoon while camping gear is unloaded. Then we climb out and tip the canoe up to tie it to the struts.

The Beaver is noisy. It rasps, growls, vibrates and hisses. But it has taken us somewhere important and so is forgiven. It has allowed us to see the way the world was, to see an ancient rainforest unmaligned.

There are 60 primary watersheds on Vancouver Island that are larger than 5000 hectares. Of these, only seven are unlogged: the Megin, Moyeha, Sydney, Power, Nasparti, East and Klaskish.

Remember those names, for they are the last.

Selected Bibliography

The 17 Year Cicada

Bonneville Power Administration. "The World's Biggest Fish Story: The Columbia River's Salmon"; "Streamline"; "Columbia River System Operation Review"; "The Columbia River: A System Under Stress"; "The Columbia River Treaty Connection"; "Rebuilding Streams For Salmon"; "Fish and Wildlife: Bringing Them Back."

Fraley, J., B. Marotsz, J. Decker-Hess, W. Beattie, and R. Zubick. *Fourth International Symposium on Regulated Streams* (selected papers), Montana Department of Fish and Wildlife, 1989.

Lindsay, R.A. "Arrow Lakes Fisheries Management Plan, 1990-1995" (draft); "Upper Arrow Reservoir Sport Fishery Statistics 1985-1986"; "Lower Arrow Reservoir Sport Fishery Statistics 1987," B.C. Ministry of the Environment.

Raymond, H.L. "Effects of hydroelectric development and fisheries enhancement on spring and summer chinook salmon and steelhead in the Columbia River basin," *North American Journal of Fisheries Management*, volume 8, 1988.

Thorp, Grant N. "Hill Creek Spawning Channel Kokanee Fry Enumeration"; "Hill Creek Rainbow Trout Brood Stock Collection," B.C. Ministry of Environment, 1988.

Ingenika Drowning

Ingenika and Mesilinka Bands. "The Ingenika And Mesilinka Story: Summary," Citizens for Public Justice, February 16, 1989.

Third Annual Electric Energy Forum. Sponsored by B.C. Hydro; Ministry of Energy, Mines and Petroleum Resources; B.C. Ministry of Environment, May 1990.

An Acceptable Level of Certainty

Ableson, D.H.G. "Omineca Fisheries: Fisheries Management Plan Upper Nechako River Watershed Including Murray and Cheslatta Lakes." B.C. Ministry of Environment, revised May 1990.

Alderdice, D.F. and G.F. Hartman. "Strangling the Nechako," in the *Fisherman*. December 17, 1990. Joint statement: "Kemano-II, The Strangulation Of Public Process And The Loss Of A River," November 25, 1990.

Burt, D.W. and J.H. Mundie. "Case Histories of Regulated Stream Flow and Its Effects On Salmonid Populations," in *Canadian Technical Report of Fisheries and Aquatic Sciences* No. 1477, Department of Fisheries and Oceans, 1986.

Department of Fisheries and Oceans. "Nechako River, British Columbia: Flow Requirements For Fish And Fish Habitat — Technical Position of the DFO." Privileged briefings prepared for counsel and departmental officials, February 10, 1986. "Toward a Fish Habitat Decision on the Kemano Completion Project: A Discussion Paper," 1984. Untitled briefing paper on Alcan and the Kemano project, April 19, 1988. "Policy For The Management of Fish Habitat," October 1986. Various news releases, 1990.

Financial Times. "Inside Story: The selling of the ambassador . . . the former Mr. Ambassador is proving adept at marketing his new enterprise: Allan Gotlieb," January 8, 1990. "Points of departure for John N. Turner," September 26, 1988.

International Pacific Salmon Fisheries Commission. "Potential Effects Of The Kemano Completion Project On Fraser River Sockeye and Pink Salmon," 1983.

Koop, Will. "Alcan Nechako-Kemano-Kitimat Development; A Chronology of Events," Rivers Defence Coalition, 1990.

Montreal *Gazette*. "What will Mila wear to fundraising ball?" February 26, 1990. "Montreal's Waldo, Beaudoin members of Order of Canada," April 13, 1989. "Business group will push deal in tour of Québec," December 12, 1987. "PM names Gotlieb as chairman of Canada Council," November 2, 1988. "Lean times ahead for B.C. Liberals," May 8, 1989. "Water supply in danger, price should rise," October 1, 1985. "PM rewards Meech Lake loyalists with Senate seats," October 1, 1988.

Morton, James. *Capilano — The Story of a River*, McClelland & Stewart, 1970.

Ottawa *Citizen*. "Partyline," January 11, 1990. "72 Canadians Share Order of Canada Honors," January 27, 1989. "Government to help industry compete in defence sector," October 6, 1987. "$94,000 spent on free-trade video," June 11, 1987. "Order of Canada recipient target of protesters," November 9, 1988. "Free-trade supporter . . . ," November 24, 1988. "No rules in groups' battle for voters," November 26, 1988. "New chairman named for Alcan," December 10, 1988. "Chairman Gotlieb: Totally wrong for Canada Council post," May 3, 1990. "Polly's People; Mila Mulroney's sports gala," September 25, 1986.

Rivers Defence Coalition. "An Analysis of the Kemano Settlement Agreement," 1988.

Settlement Agreement between Alcan, Department of Fisheries and Oceans, and the Province of British Columbia, September 14, 1987.

Toronto *Star.* "No more means tests for our senators?" December 13, 1987. "Takeovers give Big Business economic and political clout," April 5, 1986. "'Who's Who' joins fight for Meech," January 23, 1990. "Controversial free trade group reveals its 'who's who' donor list," December 9, 1989. "Ecologists cringe over Mulroney's tainted award," April 27, 1989. "Business lobby for free trade tackles deficit," February 8, 1989.

Vancouver *Sun.* "Fraser salmon at risk, Kemano papers say," December 20, 1990. "Fish flounder in the face of Alcan's clout," January 8, 1991. "Hydro switches to private sector for power needs," November 4, 1988. "The threat of the Kemano Two dam; Whoa, there," January 17, 1980. "Massive fish loss forecast if Kemano Two dam built," July 31, 1970. "Alcan water cutoff 'threatening' to kill fish," April 21, 1977. "Nechako flooding defended," June 26, 1974. "Beaver, muskrat dead, aluminum firm blamed," June 22, 1974. "Full power is 'inevitable' at Kemano power plant/Williston Hints Rejection," August 17, 1972. "Reservoir raising denied by Alcan," September 3, 1971. "Alcan May Produce War Metal in B.C.," March 20, 1951.

Moon In Its House *and* Swimming at Night

Bryan, Liz. "Backroads," in *Western Living*, August 1974.

Department of Fisheries, Biological Sciences Branch. "The Marine Survival of Salmon Program, Annual Progress Report," 1988.

Ignell, Steve. "Zonal Variability In Salmonid Drift-Net Catch Rates From Research Vessel Operations In The Central North Pacific Ocean," INPFC, U.S. National Section, October 1989.

Japan Fisheries Agency, U.S. National Marine Fisheries Service, and Department of Fisheries and Oceans. "Data Summary Of Squid And Salmon Observations In The Japanese Driftnet Fishery For Neon Flying Squid — joint report," February 1990.

Koski, K.V., Auke Bay Laboratory. "Alaska: Effects of Sediment on the Reproduction of Salmonids," National Marine Fisheries Service.

Lazeo, L. "Collectors Guide To BC Indian Artifact Sites," self-published, January 1970.

Light, Jeffrey T., Colin K. Harris, and Robert L. Burgner, Fisheries Research Institute, School of Fisheries, University of Washington. "Ocean Distribution And Migration Of Steelhead (*Oncorhynchus mykiss,* formerly *Salmo gairdneri*)," 1989.

National Oceanic and Atmospheric Administration, National Marine Fisheries Service, Office of Enforcement. "Report On High Seas Salmon Interception," January 24, 1990.

Orr, Craig. "Suspended Solids Impact On River Fish," Trout Canada.

Smith, Harlan I and Gerard Fowke. "Indian Cairns of B.C. & Washington," American Museum of Natural History, January 1901.

Teit, James A. "Tatooing And Face And Body Painting Of The Thompson Indians British Columbia," Washington Government, 1930.

Extinction and the Genetic Code

B.C. Parks Branch. Adams River background papers.

Brody, Jane E. "Water-Based Animals Are Becoming Extinct Faster Than Others," in *The New York Times*, April 23, 1991.

Department of Fisheries and Oceans. "Fraser River Sockeye Task Force, Summary Report," November 14, 1988. Adams River background material. Coho Resource Status And Management Planning Process.

Labelle, M., C.J. Walters, and B.C. Riddell, Resource Management Science, University of B.C. "Ocean survival and exploitation patterns of hatchery and wild stocks of coho salmon," Department of Fisheries and Oceans, July 1991.

Lindberg, Cheryl. "River Expedition spawns clean-up plan," in Salmon Arm *Observer*, May 1990.

Mitchell, David Salmond. "A Story of the Fraser River's Great Sockeye Run and Their Loss." Unpublished manuscript, 1925.

Nehlsen, Willa, Jack Williams, and James Lichatowich. "Pacific Salmon At The Crossroads: Stocks At Risk From California, Oregon, Idaho and Washington," American Fisheries Society, February 1991.

Oregon Trout. "Proposal For Restoration of Columbia River Salmon. Recommendations For Recovery Under The Endangered Species Act," January 1991. "Columbia Basin Anadromous Fish Extinction Record," October 1990. "Endangered Species Act Position Statement," May 1990.

Williams, Ian V., DFO, Fraser River Program. "Sockeye Salmon (*Oncorhynchus nerka*) Population Biology and Future Managment"; "Attempts to Re-Establish Sockeye Salmon (*Oncorhynchus nerka*) Populations in the Upper Adams River, British Columbia, 1949-84," Department of Fisheries and Oceans.

The Great River

Department of Fisheries and Oceans. "Pacific Region Salmon Stock Management Plan. Northern Transboundary Rivers," 1986. "Treaty Between the Government of Canada And the Government of the United States of America Concerning Pacific Salmon." "Report of the Pacific Salmon Commission Transboundary River Technical Commitee," February 8, 1987. "Report of the Canada/United States Transboundary Technical Committee," January 10, 1986. News release: "Canadian Fisheries Management Plans For The Stikine and Taku Rivers," June 1987.

Eberts, Tony. "Spatsizi Spat," in Vancouver *Province*, January 29, 1987.

Ministry of Forests. "Lower Stikine Recreation and Transportation Corridor Management Plan," February 1989. "Lower Stikine River Recreation Corridor Management Plan," December 1988.

Parks Canada, Heritage for Tomorrow. *Proceedings of the Canadian Assembly on National Parks and Protected Areas*, volume I.

Smith, David. "Aid for native fishery feared threat to firm," in Vancouver *Sun*, November 18, 1988.

Spatsizi Association For Biological Research. "Five-Year Research Program. A Prospectus," May 1988.

The Colour of Copper

Bangs, Richard and Christian Kallen. *Rivergods*, Douglas & McIntyre, 1985.

Bohn Glen. "Saving of B.C. Rivers," in Vancouver *Sun*, February 24, 1990.

Environment Canada. "Environmental Assessment and Review Process Guidelines Order," June 22, 1984.

Flather, Patti. "Big plans for Windy Craggy hinge on copper price," in *Northern Miner*, October 23, 1989.

Geddes Resources Ltd. Operational plans, January 1990. Correspondence to Mine Development Steering Committee, June 6, 1991.

Madsen, Ken and Graham Wilson. Rivers of the Yukon. Primrose Publishing, 1989.

Mining Association of British Columbia. *Windy Craggy Access Road*, volume 3, number 1, January 1990.

Tero, Richard D. "E.J. Glave and the Alsek River," in *Alaska Journal*, summer 1973.

Valley of the Grizzlies

Cox, Kevin. "Grizzly defenders warn of extinction if hunt goes ahead," in *Globe & Mail*, May 10, 1986.

Eldridge, Morely, Randy Bouchard, and Dorothy Kennedy, Millennia Research. "Khutzeymateen Ethnography and Archeology," B.C. Ministry of Municipal Affairs, December 31, 1989.

Hammond, H.L., Silva Ecosystem Consultants Ltd. "Summary Report Of Preliminary Findings Economic And Ecological Feasibility Of Forest Management In The Khutzeymateen Watershed," Friends of Ecological Reserves, March 15, 1988.

Ministry of Environment. "Khutzeymateen Study Announced," May 12, 1988. "Working Plan: Khutzeymateen Valley Grizzly Bear Study," September 1990. "Annual Progress Report — Year 1; Year 2."

Parfitt, Ben. "Tough Choices," in Vancouver *Sun*, June 18, 1991.

McCrory, Wayne. "Assessment Of Preservation Values And Opportunities For Public Viewing Of Grizzly Bears And Other Wildlife In The Proposed Khutzeymateen Grizzly Sanctuary, B.C.," Friends of Ecological Reserves, February 1987.

McCrory, Wayne, Erica Mallam. "Evaluation Of The Khutzeymateen Valley As A Grizzly Bear Sanctuary," Friends of Ecological Reserves, April 1988.

The River Guardians

B.C. Environment and Land Use Commission. "Cowichan Estuary Task Force Report," B.C. Government, 1980.

The Way The World Was

Department of Fisheries and Oceans. "Cameron River-Erosion Stream Survey and Sediment Mitigation Proposal; South Coast Division," June 4, 1986.

Friends of Clayoquot Sound. "Shark River Information Sheet," November 1990.

Forest Planning Canada. "Old Growth: A Renewable Resource, The Carmanah Story," January/February 1989.

Heritage Forests Society; Sierra Club of Western Canada. "A Proposal To Add The Carmanah Creek Drainage With Its Exceptional Sitka Spruce Forests To Pacific Rim National Park," May 1988.

International Council For Bird Preservation. "The Marbled Murrelet joins the old-growth forest conflict," in *American Birds*, summer 1988.

Johnson, Scott W., Jonathan Heifetz, and K.V. Koski. "Effects of Logging on the Abundance and Seasonal Distribution of Juvenile Steelhead in Some Southeastern Alaska Streams," Northwest and Alaska Fisheries Center, 1986.

Ministry of Forests. "Alphabetical List Of Major Unlogged Watersheds On Vancouver Island," June 12, 1990. News releases: "Marbled Murrelet Not Threatened By Logging In The Walbran," September 17, 1991. "Carmanah Lookout Deck Cause For Safety Concerns," April 11, 1990. "Short Term Deferral Of Critical Areas Of Old Growth; Recommendations of the Conservation of Areas Team Sub-Committee," September 5, 1990. "BC Parks Announces Interim Plans For Carmanah," June, 19, 1990.

Moore, Keith, Moore Resource Management. "Profiles Of The Undeveloped Watersheds On Vancouver Island: A report prepared for Friends of Ecological Reserves," February 1991. "A Preliminary Assessment of the Status of Temperate Rainforest in British Columbia: A report for Conservation International," February 1990.

Redding, Michael J. and Carl B. Schreck, Oregon Cooperative Fishery Research Unit. "Physiological Effects on Coho Salmon and Steelhead of Exposure to Suspended Solids," U.S. Fish and Wildlife Service, 1987.

U.S. Forest Service, Montana Department of Fish, Wildlife and Parks and Water Quality Bureau. "Jim Creek Monitoring," 1988-90.

Index

Adams River 97-112
Alaska Conservation Foundation 139
Alaska Department of Fish and Game 108
Alcan 33, 37, 41; Kemano Completion
  46; Kemano project 45; Kitimat alumi-
  num smelter 38, 41; links with
  Progressive Conservatives 56
Alderdice, Don 38, 48, 53, 54
Alsek River 132, 142
American Fisheries Society 111
American Rivers 132
Andrushak, Harvey 14
Arden, Chad 89
Arrow Lakes 9, 24
Audubon Society 196
B.C. Forest Products 168
B.C. government 11, 14, 33, 45, 125,
  151, 163, 197
B.C. Hydro 8, 26, 30, 33, 38, 128
B.C. Ministry of Forests 128, 129, 162,
  194-198, 200
B.C. Ministry of the Environment 26,
  82, 102, 173
Bangs, Richard 138
Bata, Sonja Ingrid 57
Beaudoin, Laurent 57
Behan, Jeff 137, 143, 150
Bendickson, D.F. 197
Bennett, W.A.C. 34

black bears 9, 21, 23, 189
Blanchard, Doug 123
Blanchard, Marilyn 123
Bloor, Bill 31
Bonneville Power Administration 13, 26
Botel, Jim 200
Boyanowsky, Ehor 70, 77
Braul, Waldemar 33
brown trout 170
Bruce, Pat 119
Burdek, John 118
Burkett, R.D. 108
Burns, Ted 178
Burt, D.W. 54
Campbell, Wayne 141
Canadian Wildlife Service 154, 197
Capilano fish hatchery 40
Capilano River 39
Carmanah Giant 187
Carmanah Pacific Provincial Park 197
Carrier Indians 28
Carrier-Sekani Tribal Council 32, 43
Cathedral Grove 191
cattle ranching 82, 84, 101
Caverly, Alan 86
Cayenne Creek 107
Chamut, Pat 48
Charette, Pierre 80
Charlie, Marvin 43

Cheslatta band 33, 43; displacement 44
Cheslatta Falls 53
chinook 11, 39, 46, 50, 100, 116, 135, 172
Choquette Glacier 114
Clayoquot Sound 186, 201
Cleveland Dam 39
coho 39, 100, 116, 119, 124, 144, 171, 179; lake and stream 180
Columbia River 3-26
Columbia River Power System 11
Columbia River Treaty 11
Cominco 3, 7, 20, 127
Connell, Harry 7, 13
Conservation International 186, 193
Cooper, John 142
Cowichan Lake 168
Cowichan Lake Salmonid Enhancement Society 178
Cowichan River 167-183
Crispin, Jim 20
Culver, David 57
cutthroat trout 111, 170, 190, 204
Dalton, Jack 135
dams: Columbia River 8, 25; compensation 32; Cowichan Lake weir 168, 175; environmental costs 25, 28, 38, 42; flooding 27; Iskut River 128; social costs 31, 44; Stikine River 128; water levels 21, 28, 38, 167
Deadman Chasm Steelhead Sanctuary 93
Deadman River 79-95, 104
DeBeck, Howard 45
Department of Fisheries and Oceans (DFO) 12, 37, 46-47, 54, 103, 106, 121, 171, 191, 198; northern fisheries region 114
Department of Indian Affairs 33
Didlick, Nick 77, 135, 140, 143
Docksteader, Pauline 94
Dolly Varden 9
Douglas fir 168, 187, 193
Dudgeon, Greg 146
Dunn, Sean 88
Ennis, Gordon 12
Environment Youth Corps 103
erosion 61, 189, 192, 199
extinction 98, 103, 109, 111
Finlay River 28, 30

fish: "slime" 87; fry 94, 108; gas supersaturation 13, 54; gene stock 49, 65, 88, 99, 111; gene stock replacement 108; pollution 4, 19, 73, 127, 145; salmon 63; spawning 52, 101; trout 202; water levels 21, 46, 49, 54, 72, 90, 101, 167, 170-71, 174, 179; water temperature 52, 55, 90, 101, 171
fish hatcheries 9, 12, 26, 40, 49, 56, 112, 125
fish stocks survey 111
Fisheries Act 47, 92, 192
fishery enhancement 13, 16, 38, 48, 51, 54, 103, 107, 109, 112, 123, 172, 176, 178
fishery losses 9, 11, 39, 54, 64, 98, 109, 111, 172, 181, 190, 202
fishing: commercial 12, 65, 70, 98, 117, 118, 145; native 12, 66, 103, 135; sport 4, 12, 13, 18, 22, 62, 73, 75, 76, 135, 167; transboundary 116; U.S. 116
Fletcher Challenge Canada Ltd. 168, 170, 177, 202
Foster, Hoyt 195
Fox, Rosemary 129
Fraser River 8, 38, 50, 53, 65, 98, 106, 122
Fraser River Advisory Commission 66
Friends of Clayoquot Sound 187
Friends of the Stikine 125, 127
Geddes Resources Ltd. 132, 136, 140, 145
Gitsees Indians 158
Glacier Bay National Park and Preserve 132, 146
Glave, Edward James 135, 138
Goodwin, Jack 146
Gotlieb, Allan 57
Gould, Bob 120
Grand Canyon (Stikine) 113, 128
Great Glacier 114
Great Glacier Salmon co-op 118, 120
grizzly bears 21, 24, 142, 153-166
Haig-Brown, Roderick 39
Haimas, George 156
Hammond, Herb 162
Hartman, Gordon 38, 48, 53
Hell's Gate 98, 106

Heritage Forests Society 187
Heywood, Dave 170
Horney, Ralph 18
Hume, Andrew 131
Hume, Timothy 195
Ingenika band 27, 30, 31
Interior Indian Fisheries Commission 66
International Biological Program 162
International Council for Bird Preservation 196
International Pacific Salmon Fisheries Commission 106
irrigation 90, 101
Isaac, Francis 30, 31
Isaac, Jean 27
Iskut River 123, 125, 127, 128
Izony, Ray 34
Jacob, Stephan 120, 122
John, Ed 33
Jonini, Harry 41
Junell, Joseph 43
Kallen, Christian 138
Karluk Lake 108
Kateen River 159
Kemano project 37, 38; history 45
Kenney Dam 41, 42
Khutzeymateen River 153-166
Kinbasket Lake 8
Kirkby, Ken 71, 74, 77
Kluane National Park 132
Klukshu River 135, 137
Knudson, Tom 143
Koenings, J.P. 108
Koop, Will 45
Kraft, R.W. 53
Kujala, Stan 199
Kyuquot Economic and Environmental Protection Society 199
Lawson, Steve 201
Leachty, Carey 67
LeConte Wilderness Area 125
logging 61, 127-29 154, 162, 170, 180, 186, 197; clearcutting 128, 188; environmental costs 189, 193, 198
Loup Creek 198
Lower Stikine River Recreational Corridor Management Plan 128
MacMillan Bloedel 191, 197, 202

Madsen, Ken 138
Mallette, Alphonse 16
Mallette, Greg 16
Mallam, Erica 154, 160
Malloway, Ken 66
marbled murrelet 189, 195
McCrory, Wayne 153, 159, 163
McGregor, Ian 82, 91
McIntyre, Kerry 19
McNall, Michael 142
McSpadden, Ralph 146
Megin River 194-205
mines 124, 126-127, 132, 144-145
Ministry of Agriculture 102
Mitchell, Bob 19
Mitchell, David Salmond 97
Momich River 108
Moore, Dave 103
Moore, Keith 186
Morton, James 40
Moyeha River 194, 202
Mulroney, Brian 56
Mundie, J.H. 54
Munn, Jim 129
Murphy Creek 14
Myers, Eric 148
Nanika River 45
Nechako River 37-59
Nechako River Working Group 48
Nelson, Leo 182
Newall, J.E. 57
Nicola River 61
Niemi, Nels 139, 147
Nyland, Jim 46
Old Growth Strategy Project 194
Ootsa Lake 43
Oregon Natural Resources Council 197
Peace River 27-35
Pearse, Peter 58
Pedersen, Dale 20
Peel, Nancy 139, 143, 149
Peel, Robert 148
Pelleet, Pat 146
Pierre, Gordon 34
Poitras, Jean-Marie 57
pollution: Columbia River 4, 19; Iskut River 127; Stikine River 127; Tatshenshini River 145; Thompson River 73

radio tracking: bears 154, 159; fish 84
rainbow trout 4, 9, 14, 63, 85, 170
Reid, Don 66
Reid, George 173
Residents for a Free-Flowing Stikine 125
Rich, Willis 111
Richmond, Claude 196
river rafting 131, 134, 136, 146
river restoration 82, 92, 102, 103, 106, 178
riverbank deterioration 82, 83, 90, 92, 101, 180, 191
Rivers Defence Coalition 50
road construction 144, 146, 162, 189; erosion 200
Roderick Haig-Brown Conservation Area 105
Rowlands, Peter 127, 130
Russell, Dick 154, 160
Salmon Arm 97
Salmon Arm Bay Nature Enhancement Society 102
Salmon Arm Fish and Game Club 100, 102
Salmon River 97-112
Salmon River Project 102, 104
Saysell, Joe 167, 170, 175
sedimentation 90, 92, 101, 181, 189, 191
Sekani Indians 28
Shark River 203
Shinners, Wayne 37
Shuswap Advocates for Youth 102
Shuswap Lake 97
Shuswap Nation Tribal Council 102
Siddon, Tom 37, 49
Sieffert, Bruce 162
Sierra Club 129, 187
Sitka spruce 154, 187
Smith, Paul 145
Snetsinger, Jim 129
sockeye 50, 51, 98, 135, 153
Spatsizi Provincial Park 125
Spences Bridge 61, 75
spring salmon 40
steelhead 11, 39, 62, 87, 119, 173, 202; commercially intercepted 65; fry 90, 93; gene stock 72; migrating 64 76, 79, 84; spawning 86, 93; taxonomy 63
Steelhead Society of B.C. 70

Stephen, John R. 198
Stepp, John 76
Stikine National Park Reserve 125
Stikine River 113-130
Straight, Lee 67
Strangway, David 37
Strathcona Park 194, 202
Stratton, Jim (Stratto) 139, 144, 148
Tahltan Indians 114, 118, 121
Tahsish River 200
Tats Creek 147
Tatshenshini River 131-151; commercial fishing 117
Tauber, Dave 123
Teit, James 68
temperate rainforest 186, 193
Thompson Indians 67, 69
Thompson River 61-78, 79, 103; steelhead stock 64, 84, 85
Tlingit Indians 113, 158
Trail Wildlife Association 14
transboundary rivers 116
Tsimshian Indians 158
Tsuyuki, Henry 71
Turkii, Pat 43
Tutty, Brian 172, 175
U.S. Fish and Wildlife Service 197
U.S. Forest Service 190
U.S. Water Quality Bureau 190
Ululame'llst, Baptiste 69
Upper Adams River 105-112
W.A.C. Bennett Dam 28
Walbran Valley 196, 198
Western Canada Wilderness Committee 187, 197
Western Forest Industries 198
Wightman, Craig 173, 175
Williams, Ian 106, 110
Williston Lake 27, 30
Williston, Ray 34
Wilson, Graham 138
Wilson, Michael 57
Windy Craggy Mountain 134, 144
Woods, Cal 70
Yule, Darcy 200
Zealand, Gordon 116

Caring for Wilderness in Canada

The Canadian Parks and Wilderness Society envisages a healthy ecosphere where people experience and respect natural ecosystems. We believe that by ensuring the health of the parts, we ensure the health of the whole, which is our health too. This book is part of the Society's Henderson Book Series, an exciting series of conservation books that includes titles such as *Endangered Spaces* edited by conservationist Monte Hummel and *Home Place: Essays on Ecology* by well-known ecologist Stan Rowe. The Society has nine chapters across Canada. In addition to conservation programs such as Endangered Spaces, the society also publishes *Borealis* magazine, a leading magazine about nature, the environment and wilderness.

Join the Canadian Parks and Wilderness Society and you will be helping save endangered spaces right across Canada. You will also receive a subscription to *Borealis* quarterly magazine. Inside you will find dramatic, lively, colorful, hard-hitting coverage of environmental issues in Canada.

To enrol as a member, enclose payment of $31 (by cheque, VISA or MC) payable to the Canadian Parks and Wilderness Society. Please provide your full name, address and postal code. If you are paying by VISA or Mastercard, please indicate which card you are using, indicate you are paying $31, sign the letter and include your card number and expiry date.

CANADIAN PARKS and WILDERNESS SOCIETY

Suite 1335, 160 Bloor Street East
Toronto, Ontario M4W 1B9
(416)972-0868